NO MATTER H... SMOKING ... CIGARETTES Y... PETRIE METHO... ...JUST LIKE IT HAS HELPED THOUSANDS BEFORE YOU:

"Excellent... it got me to stop smoking almost painlessly."

—J.A., New York, NY
20 cigarettes a day, 21-year habit

"I never knew it could be so easy. If asked, I would recommend your program to everyone who wants to quit."

—M.M., Quincy, MA
25–30 cigarettes a day, 24-year habit

"I'm thrilled with the results. I feel much better and seldom think of a cigarette. My friends and family are amazed."

—L.L., Jersey Shore, PA
20 cigarettes a day, 15-year habit

"I'm so delighted that your program has worked so well for me, I have only compliments to offer."
—E.C., New York, NY
25–30 cigarettes a day, 14-year habit

"I already feel like a 'new' person. This method is superior to any other.... My sincere appreciation."
—F.V., North Bergen, NJ
50 cigarettes a day, 25-year habit

"It worked! Thank you very, very much!"
—S.K., North Bellmore, NY
20 cigarettes a day, 18-year habit

• • •

Copies of these and other signed testimonials are on file and may be examined at Warner Books, 666 Fifth Avenue, New York, NY 10103.

Also by Sidney Petrie

How to Stop Smoking in Three Days

Published by
WARNER BOOKS

ATTENTION: SCHOOLS AND CORPORATIONS

WARNER books are available at quantity discounts with bulk purchase for educational, business, or sales promotional use. For information, please write to: SPECIAL SALES DEPARTMENT, WARNER BOOKS, 666 FIFTH AVENUE, NEW YORK, N.Y. 10103.

**ARE THERE WARNER BOOKS
YOU WANT BUT CANNOT FIND IN YOUR LOCAL STORES?**

You can get any WARNER BOOKS title in print. Simply send title and retail price, plus 50¢ per order and 50¢ per copy to cover mailing and handling costs for each book desired. New York State and California residents add applicable sales tax. Enclose check or money order only, no cash please, to: WARNER BOOKS, P.O. BOX 690, NEW YORK, N.Y. 10019.

HOW TO STOP SMOKING IN 3 HOURS

SIDNEY PETRIE
Founder of the New York Institute for Hypnotherapy and author of *How to Stop Smoking in 3 Days*
DAVID PETRIE
Director of Hypnosis Habit Control Systems
with **JULIE HOUSTON**

WARNER BOOKS

A Warner Communications Company

"This program is not intended as a substitute for medical advice. You are advised to consult regularly with your health care professional in matters relating to your health, and particularly regarding matters which may require diagnosis or medical attention."

Please call if you have any questions or comments.

WARNER BOOKS EDITION

Copyright © 1989 by the Estate of Sidney Petrie and David Petrie
All rights reserved.

Cover design by Mike Stromberg

Warner Books, Inc.
666 Fifth Avenue
New York, N.Y. 10103

 A Warner Communications Company

Printed in the United States of America

First Printing: March, 1989

10 9 8 7 6 5 4 3 2

To the memory of my father, Sidney,
who exerted his own
very special hypnotic influence over me.

SIDNEY PETRIE, noted hypnotherapist, author, and lecturer was the founder and director of the New York Institute for Hypnotherapy. For his contributions to the field of behavioral conditioning through hypnosis, he received honorary doctorates in science and the humanities. He was also a member of the American Psychotherapy Association and an associate fellow of the American College of Clinical Hypnosis.

DAVID PETRIE is a practicing hypnotherapist and the director of Hypnosis Control Systems in Great Neck, New York. He is also a member of the New York State Association for Counseling and Development.

Contents

Foreword	xi
Introduction	1
How to Use this Book	5
Transferring Scripts to Audio Tape	7

THE FIRST HOUR: Preparing for Self-Hypnosis — 9

1 Helping Yourself to a Healthy Slice of Life — 11
2 Knowing Yourself Is Important — 22
3 It's Time to Finally Kick the Habit — 32
4 Preparing to Stop Smoking Forever — 41
5 How to Stop Smoking Without Gaining Weight — 49

THE SECOND HOUR: Practicing Self-Hypnosis — 65

6 Understanding the Value of the Relaxation Response — 67
7 Hypnosis and Self-Hypnosis— A Powerful Force for Good — 77

THE THIRD HOUR: Putting Hypnosis to Work for You—Now It's Time to Quit — 95

8 Your Hour to Stop Smoking — 97
9 The New, Nonsmoking You— Adjusting to Being a Healthy Ex-Smoker — 117
10 Ensuring Your Long-Term Success as an Ex-Smoker — 128

Foreword

As the director of a consulting firm specializing in helping people develop life/self-management skills, I have contact with a variety of clients—people just like you—who have the desire to improve the quality of their lives. For most of my clients, giving up smoking is one of their most important goals. For example:

- A business administrator who is responsible for enforcing a no-smoking policy in his office and recognizes that he must set the example for his co-workers by no longer smoking.

- A teacher who personally concludes that smoking is disgusting, unhealthy, time consuming, expensive, and annoying to his friends and associates that do not smoke.

- A parent who realizes that the smoke he is exhaling throughout his home is polluting the air and is unhealthy for his wife and children to breathe.

- A pregnant woman who has been warned by her doctor that her smoking may be harmful to her unborn child.

To improve my techniques as a consultant and to meet the needs of my clients, I participated in a training workshop to learn the Petrie Method.® The seminar was conducted at the

Institute for Hypnotherapy by a Petrie-certified hypnotherapist. Participants were doctors, psychologists, nurses, social workers, and counselors. Our purpose for attending was to learn how to use the Petrie Method to facilitate health-promoting changes in the lives of our clients.

Since taking the workshop, I have been using the Petrie Method with my clients, and the results have been highly successful, particularly with smokers. After one office visit and a brief follow-up period using the Petrie Quit-Smoking Tape on a regular basis, my clients have reported that they are no longer smoking and they feel 100 percent better. Because of their success, they are referring their friends and business associates to me.

Now, for the first time, the expertise that formerly was only available through private or group sessions with a certified Petrie hypnotherapist is available for you to use in the privacy of your home. After reading this short book and following the procedures prescribed, you will be able to use hypnosis to change your life-style. Although the guided instructions are specifically designed to inhibit smoking, the skills that you develop can also be transferred to weight control and stress management.

Hypnotherapists Sidney and David Petrie are to be commended for sharing these highly successful hypnosis techniques. For over thirty years, the Petrie Method has enabled hundreds of thousands of people to live happier and healthier lives. Without reservation, I recommend that you read this book, follow the instructions, and quit smoking for life. It's the only one you have. You might as well live it in good health.

> Dr. Marianne B. Lally
> Director
> Potential Development Associates International
> Northport, New York

Introduction

You are about to change your life forever—to make it healthier, happier, and more rewarding than you ever thought possible. Your innermost wish to stop smoking—a wish that until now you may have abandoned in despair—is about to come true. *Three relaxing hours* are all you need to make it happen—to overcome your powerful craving for cigarettes once and for all. It doesn't matter whether you've smoked twenty cigarettes a day for the last thirty years, or two packs a day for the last ten, or three cigarettes a day for the last twenty years. *You are going to quit smoking now.*

The three-hour program presented in this book is unlike any other quit-smoking program that exists today. It is based on the Petrie Method, an easy-to-learn process of self-hypnosis that was developed in the 1950s by my father, Sidney Petrie, who was far ahead of his time in recognizing the benefits of hypnosis in treating addictions.

Hypnotherapy is a proven, powerful tool that can not only reshape your attitude toward smoking, (making you more receptive to the dangers of the habit), but can also create a mental block, or barrier, that prevents you from acting upon your cravings. If you have ever relied on will power to quit smoking, you know the difficulties. For most people, will power is simply not strong enough to overcome their smoking addiction. That is why the Petrie Method relies on another, more dependable area of your mind—your subconscious—to cure your cigarette addiction through suggestions that are made on a subconscious level. This fascinating process is detailed later on in the book. But for now, you need only know that the Petrie Method is able to break the cycle of addiction for more smokers—average people just like you and me—than any other stop-smoking program that I know of.

Times have changed since my father founded the Institute for Hypnotherapy in 1957 and introduced his specialized hypnosis techniques to the general public in group and individual hypnotherapy sessions. Hypnosis, or self-hypnosis—terms which are used interchangeably in this book—has gained a broad and solid reputation for some remarkable accomplishments. Today it is hailed by the American Medical Association (AMA) as a useful technique in treating a wide variety of conditions. It is used as a substitute for pain control in surgical procedures and in childbirth; for treating skin disorders and other physical ailments; for helping develop self-confidence; and for controlling addictions, which is the objective of our simple and effective program.

So if you are ready to put aside just three hours of your time to follow this safe, relaxing self-hypnosis program, you will discover what hundreds of thousands of average men and women attending the Petrie Method Quit-Smoking Seminar have discovered—that there really is a safe, simple, and extraordinarily effective method of breaking free from the bonds of your smoking habit. With the Petrie Method, you can stop smoking *permanently*—without the anxiety and discomfort you may now connect with the mere thought of quitting smoking, without the cravings and mood swings you may anticipate—and *without gaining a pound*!

Contrary to what many people envision, you won't go to sleep when using self-hypnosis. Nor will you be unconscious or in any way out of control. Instead, you will experience a sense of well-being, safety, and comfort that you may never have known. At the same time, you will enjoy the supreme satisfaction, the sheer exhilaration, that comes from taking control of your smoking addiction without props, and getting rid of it *forever*.

How the Petrie Method Quit-Smoking Program Evolved —And Why It Is Tailor-made for Today

Thirty years ago, developing a hypnotherapy program as a means to stop smoking seemed feasible because of the great success of hypnotic suggestion with weight control. At the time, smoking was not as widely recognized as a harmful addiction as it is today. Participation in the program was limited to people with smoking-related illnesses who had been referred by the medical profession which, to this day, has yet to be completely successful in helping patients quit smoking, or lose weight and keep it off. Drawing from the existing approach we used for weight loss and addiction to drugs and alcohol, we formulated a methodology under which hypnosis could be used to help smokers break free from their dependency on cigarettes. Ironically, while the methods worked wonders in helping people deal with other addictions, the program was not successful with smokers—at least, not at first. We didn't realize that smoking was different from other addictions, which can be treated on a weekly basis, over a period of time. Smokers who continued to smoke between sessions (as invariably was the case) only readdicted themselves and reinforced their habit. We knew we had to come up with an intensified program that would present all the information and guidance the smoker needed to quit—*in one session*. This was our big breakthrough. We changed the format from ongoing sessions to one session, and immediately doubled our success rate.

Perfecting the program was also perfectly timed. Soon

afterward came the Surgeon General's warnings, and people who wanted to stop smoking but couldn't do it on their own came to us in droves for help. We were ready for them. And now that newer, more stringent no-smoking laws are being adopted all across the country, we are ready for *you*.

Based on questionnaires that are returned to us from the participants in our quit-smoking program, we know we're doing something right. Those who have stated that they have permanently quit smoking add up to an astounding 82 to 85 percent, with the even more remarkable fact that of those 10 or 15 percent who fail to achieve their goal, nearly all would *still* recommend the program to others.

This book, then, is the culmination of many years' work with hundreds of thousands of people who have quit smoking with the Petrie Method. Our original stop-smoking program has been amended, updated, and so finely tuned that if you follow what you read, you can, with conviction, stop smoking in three hours. You will find here exactly what you would find in all our seminars—a carefully formatted approach to end your smoking addiction, based on clear, step-by-step, *proven* methodology. Each of the parts of the program leads naturally to the next—from preparing, to practicing, to putting hypnosis to work for you in achieving your status as an ex-smoker.

With hypnosis, there are no surprises; things don't happen suddenly. You rehearse each step of the way to reach your goal. And if you will let yourself go, let yourself enjoy three hours of pleasant relaxation, you will not only reach your goal, but will also enjoy the process more than you could have imagined.

You have the means to quit smoking right here in your hands. Let's begin—with a promise to yourself that this time, you're really going to do it.

David Petrie

How to Use this Book

Right now, as you are reading this page—and before you read any further—I want you to commit yourself in writing to a Quitting Day that will occur within two weeks of today. Quitting Day is important not for what day it is, but rather because it adds momentum, and a focal point, to your preparations to quit. There's no such thing as a "good Tuesday" or a "good Sunday." Obviously, if you are going to have an operation on Wednesday, Tuesday would be a very poor choice of a day to try to quit smoking. And while you would think vacations would be a prime, stress-free time to quit, we've found it's just the opposite—possibly because cigarettes are often part and parcel of the smoker's picture of a leisurely vacation.

Make your commitment in writing on the next page. Note it down in your date book, or on your wall calendar, or tape it to the mirror in the bathroom—wherever a reminder of it will stand out. Discuss it with friends and colleagues. This is your firm commitment—an unbreakable promise to yourself that you will begin the program on that date.

A day or two before Quitting Day, transfer the hypnotic exercises onto two audio tapes, following the guidelines given on page 7.

On Quitting Day, at your appointed time, start reading this book from page 9 through until the end. When you conclude your reading, you will be an ex-smoker.

MY COMMITMENT TO MYSELF:

I, _____, do promise that on _____
                                           cut-off date

starting at _____ I will spend three uninterrupted hours
           A.M./P.M.
following the program in this book to quit smoking.

Transferring Scripts to Audio Tape

The relaxation and hypnotic exercises are presented in script format so that they can be recorded on audio tape and played back when called for in the program. In the time between setting the date to quit and sitting down to begin the three-hour program, you should record these exercises on tape in the same order as they are presented in this book. (They appear on pages 69, 84, 89, 99, and 107. The last two go on a separate tape.) Then, when your quit-smoking session is underway, you will be free to close your eyes and concentrate on the hypnosis.

Making your own audio tapes can be just as effective a means of self-hypnosis as the techniques used by trained hypnotherapists in our sessions. It is easy if you speak slowly and distinctly when reading the scripts, and pause (counting silently to three) at the end of each sentence and where you see a space in the text. Familiarize yourself with the exercises before taping them. Read each one aloud first, making note of the special taping guidelines that may accompany it. Relax as you speak. Pace yourself so that the time it takes to make your taping is approximately the same amount of time suggested with each exercise. Pause between the exercises and be sure to identify them by name (Hypnotic Exercise 1, etc.) and book page, for identification. You should tape the exercises ahead, but remember, do not read any other sections of the book before your Quitting Day.

THE FIRST HOUR:
Preparing for Self-Hypnosis

Now your own personal three-hour session begins. Welcome. And congratulations for keeping your appointment—your commitment to yourself.

In preparing to use self-hypnosis, you don't need to *do* anything. Simply read the next five chapters and *think carefully* about what they contain. Each chapter introduces certain topics related to smoking that bolster the case against cigarettes and help clarify your firm commitment to quit. Let what you read sink in. Have a pencil and paper handy and, of course, your pretaped hypnotic exercises. While the success of your hypnosis does not depend entirely on the information presented in these opening chapters, you'll have a better chance of achieving your goal if you read this part of the book first.

So get comfortable, put the phone off the hook, settle down into your favorite chair, and let's begin.

1

Helping Yourself to a Healthy Slice of Life

How often do you open a new pack of cigarettes, and something inside of you says "I know I shouldn't smoke?" But nevertheless, you go ahead and take a cigarette, deliberately light it, and begin to puff away, feeling guilty as can be.

What are you feeling guilty about? The probable answer is that for that instant, you are placing more importance on that cigarette than you are on your own self-image and health—even your very life. It is this compulsive act that hypnosis will change today. By the time you are finished reading this book, your self-image, your health, and your life span will *always* take precedence over that cigarette.

Because using hypnosis to stop smoking is new to you, you probably cannot quite yet believe in its effects. This is normal. If, for example, you were fearful of flying and expected to be terrified when the plane taxied down the runway (the very picture of it bringing sweat to your palms and a knot in your stomach), it would be hard to convince you as you stood on the ground that hypnosis could get you to fly in a plane without the slightest fear or anxiety. With hypnosis you could be convinced, but you would never discover how peacefully and calmly you could fly unless you bought a ticket and boarded a plane. With this book, you have bought a ticket, as it were, on the nonsmoking express, but to reach your goal, *you must climb aboard*. No one can push you on. No one can make you do anything that you do not want to do. If you put this book down and light a cigarette, don't expect a hand to come out of the heavens and snatch it out of your mouth. *You* are the one responsible for your commitment to quit. However, by participating in the hypnotic exercises presented during the next three hours, you will not want to light that cigarette, nor will you have the desire to do so. Again, all it takes is your cooperation, your total participation, and your absolute commitment.

As for the motivation to quit, never before has there been such an urgency *not* to smoke.

Until now, the strongest case against smoking has been a medical one—a case many smokers choose to ignore. They know very well what the inherent dangers are; they simply deny that they would be affected by them. But when the dangers are introduced during hypnosis, something interesting happens: Suddenly, they become very real, assuming a much higher, more intense level of importance for the individual. In hypnosis, the smoker accepts the risks for what they are—a very real threat to his or her health—and puts them in their proper place as a prime motivation to quit.

The newest findings on cigarettes reveal a far more pervasive, harmful influence on the body than the all-too-familiar health scares of the past. Information on this appears later in this chapter. But let us imagine for the moment that there is no such thing as a health risk and turn instead to a significant new factor that has emerged in the case against smoking—a curious phenomenon that offers a more compelling reason to quit the habit than all those unseen dangers you read about:

Smoking is no longer the fashionable thing to do.

Public opinion has made such a complete about-face that those who are still lighting up find themselves in the uncomfortable position of supporting what is now a socially unacceptable and offensive habit. This sudden unacceptability adds an ironic twist to the image of being a smoker. Where once there was social pressure to smoke, now there is social pressure *not* to smoke!

There are several reasons why the tides have suddenly turned against smoking. One of them has to do with image, of course, and the standard of youthful energy and fitness millions of Americans have aspired to since the days when Kennedy was president. In connection with this image, cigarette advertising compaigns cleverly paired smoking with a sporty, outdoor life style. The radiant beauty leaning out over the side of the pool, lighting up a cigarette; the rugged individual on horseback, eyes trained on the horizon and cigarette dangling from his lips—these selling images convinced a receptive public that it was glamorous, macho, and sexy to smoke.

But then the message was tested against reality, by many of those very same people who bought the cigarettes.

Ordinary men and women began to get serious about their own personal fitness, leaving behind sedentary life styles and taking up regular exercise. Smokers joined health clubs just as quickly as everyone else, only to discover that physical fitness and the abusive habit of smoking don't mix. The body won't allow it. Forced to choose between jogging, working out in the gym, or playing tennis on a regular basis—and smoking—more people today have given up their smoking habit because of personal fitness goals than for any other reason.

There's added reinforcement—the Surgeon General's warning of the serious health risks involved in smoking that is printed on every pack of cigarettes. This relays a strong health message that should bolster the determination of every smoker-turned-fitness buff. In fact, the documented truths about what cigarettes can do to your body should be enough to make anyone quit. But the tobacco industry is very cagey; it will do anything to get you to keep buying its products—even if it means finding new ways to twist the truth.

Up until the mid-1950s, there were no truth-in-advertising laws—the tobacco industry could say anything it wanted to say. Glance through old magazines from the 1940s and you will see such untruthful claims as, "More doctors smoke Camels than any other cigarette because Camels create the T-zone of smoothness. T for taste. T for your throat." There were loads of such ads, and while they no longer exist, and we now know about the dangers of smoking that we did not know then, there is still evidence that the tobacco industry couldn't care less about your health. Take the example of the "light" cigarette. There used to be a commercial demonstrating how many particles of tar, nicotine, and other waste residues could be filtered out of one puff of smoke, blown into a handkerchief. Well, you are inhaling that garbage into your lungs, regardless of what filter you use. Every cigarette, including even the "lightest" brand, contains over two hundred identifiable poisons—tar and nicotine, but also arsenic, cyanide, formaldehyde, carbon dioxide, carbon monoxide, and phenol. And if you think they are present in such minor quantities that they won't affect your health, let me set you straight. By smoking one pack a day, you would, at the end of one year, put approximately a quart of tar into your lungs—whether you deny it or not!

When the FCC banned cigarette ads from television and radio nearly twenty years ago, the tobacco industry came up with a brilliant idea. They researched the list of poisons and found that the easiest thing to lower in cigarettes would be its tars—but that removing the tar took away from the taste. The marketing people decided, who cares about the taste? What the public wants is a healthier cigarette. So they came out with "light" cigarettes, and then they came out with "ultra light" cigarettes—all the time knowing that "lights" were no better for you than ordinary filtered cigarettes.

Ten years after "light" cigarettes were introduced, the Surgeon General published a study documenting that there wasn't 1/10 of 1 percent difference in the contents of filtered and "light" filtered cigarettes. If anything, people smoking "light" cigarettes were worse off because they inhaled much deeper than people who smoked regular filtered cigarettes, and when they switched to "lights," most people increased their smoking—their "daily dose of nicotine"—by one third.

So what was the real success of the "light" campaign? Simply *selling more cigarettes to the same people*.

Profit alone motivates the tobacco industry, and as the heat intensifies in this country to exercise tighter control over how cigarettes are sold and to give more explicit warnings about what they contain, the tobacco companies simply reach out for new markets overseas and in Third World countries. There, they can create new nicotine addicts, without breaking the law by removing warnings from their packaging!

Make no mistake: While the ad campaigns would still have you believe that healthy individuals smoke, the image of that healthy individual being a smoker is no longer a credible one. Today, it's the nonsmoker, the ex-smoker—the individual who's "cleaned up his or her act" and quit smoking—who represents the image of health and success, and gains the respect of his peers. Flip through the pages of a magazine like *Esquire* or *Fortune* and you can see the kind of healthy, strapping individuals who embody what is fashionable today. They're the people who have made it to the top of the corporate world, photographed in their lavish offices in midtown Manhattan—or working out in the gym. *Smoking clearly has no place in the image of success that they project.*

Further proof that smoking is *out* lies in the current buildup of the antismoking campaign—a virtual battle between nonsmokers and smokers that was unheard of just a few years ago. The newly documented knowledge that "secondary smoke"—the smoke that is released into the environment and inhaled by smoker and nonsmoker alike—is a health hazard, has caused immediate resistance to smoking in public places. Nonsmokers who were once timid about asking smokers to "put it out" (a request that was viewed as impolite), have become positively assertive, if not aggressive, in demanding a smoke-free atmosphere.

The pressure is on and every smoker feels it—in restaurants, airports, waiting rooms, and hotels; in public buildings and public spaces everywhere. Airlines now have no-smoking rules on trips under two hours. Even in places where smoking is permitted, nonsmokers who are close by will still object—ostentatiously fanning the air and making the smoker feel uncomfortable. *Smokers are becoming segregated from society—put into smoking compartments, as it were; treated as second-class citizens.*

While the antismoking campaign is inescapable, the effect it has on smokers varies. For some, it's simply a nuisance—moving to another table in a restaurant, sitting in a special section on a plane. They'll comply with the new regulations, knowing they can retreat back to the privacy of their homes for a comfortable atmosphere in which to smoke. But for others, like yourself, the unacceptability of the smoking habit has become intensely real. These are people who are suddenly faced with a new situation or event in their lives—something that adds a new urgency to their need to quit.

- They begin dating a person who can't stand smoking, and are faced with either giving up cigarettes or risking the loss of romance.

- They find their long-sought dream apartment—and it is available to nonsmokers only.
- They're offered a long-awaited career opportunity—and smoking on this job is out.

Insidious things are happening. More and more applications for major corporations include the question, "Do you smoke?" And if the department head who's hiring is a violent antismoker, or doesn't like cigarettes, the applicant who smokes may well be bypassed for that reason alone, regardless of his or her credentials. More often, smokers can't even get a foot in the door. It may not be legal, but that's the way things are. Check the classified ads in the newspapers and see how frequently they specify nonsmokers—in the personal columns, the employment pages, and real estate sections. Once again, it reflects the trend that *if you are a smoker today, you are out of place*.

At the root of all this social pressure is *health*. The collective conscience of our society demands that smokers no longer ignore the proven risks of smoking, and if they're not going to quit for themselves, they must do so for the well-being of their families, friends, and co-workers.

The Destiny of Your Health and Life Is Primarily in Your Hands

The human body is totally dependent on the wiles of its owner. The caring, health-oriented individual treats his or her body as it would treat a good friend—protecting it, nurturing it, thinking always about its well-being. On the other hand, the smoker betrays that friendship with every cigarette smoked.

We have a much more sophisticated knowledge of the effects of smoking on the body than we did in the past. We know that nicotine affects a major neurotransmitter system involved in the conduction of nerve signals, memory, and other critical functions. It also binds onto white blood cells and is carried to most tissues throughout the body. This is important information, in light of the fact that, as explained earlier, tobacco contains over two hundred poisonous substances. By smoking, all these poisons permeate the body.

Every year new findings about the effects of smoking come to light, and the notion that *any* existing conditon is exacerbated by smoking has indeed become a credible one. Dermatologists, for example, have confirmed that most eruptive skin conditions, such as acne, are adversely affected by smoking. They know that smoking encourages advanced aging of the skin.

Moreover, because more women smoke today than they did in the past, a whole new body of health risks linked to smoking has come to light. In 1986, lung cancer surpassed breast cancer as the number one cancer killer of women. Smoking during pregnancy increases the chance of premature birth, miscarriage, and sudden infant death syndrome. Intrauterine pictures show with startling clarity the effects of smoking on an unborn baby's circulatory system. The mother inhales one or two puffs of a cigarette and the delicate network of capillaries in the baby's fingers constrict, their blood supply decreasing and temporarily disappearing from view. If this is happening in the baby's fingers, one might ask what is happening in the baby's brain? A female smoker who uses birth control pills has ten times the normal risk of a heart attack and twenty times the risk of a cerebral hemorrhage. Smoking is now also linked to early menopause. On and on the new facts and statistics are published; next year, we'll undoubtedly discover more of them.

The evidence of the damaging effect of cigarettes on the respiratory system growns grimmer every year. Lung cancer, with a cure rate of less than 10 percent, and emphysema, with its irreversible damage to lung tissue, are two of the more familiar illnesses linked to smoking—tragic when the smoker might have prevented them by quitting.

We know that *all* smokers run an extra risk of heart and circulatory diseases; the medical data indirectly connecting smoking with arteriosclerosis, strokes, heart attacks, and other illnesses is now academic. All are revealed with chilling clarity in slides and photographs: Lungs collapsed with emphysema, or discolored with cancer. Gums with gingivitis, or afflicted with ulcers from chewing tobacco. Cancers of the lip, or the inside of the cheek. Cancer of the larynx and the bladder.

"Oh, but that only happens to heavy smokers, not me!" you've probably said to yourself. But the fact of the matter is that *everyone* who smokes is at risk, as well as those around them.

A two-pack-a-day smoker shortens his life by an average of eight years; but even the light smoker, who smokes one to nine cigarettes daily, shortens his life expectancy by approximately four years.

A one-pack-a-day smoker puts approximately one quart of tobacco tars into his or her lungs every year—sticky, chemical-laden tars that accumulate on the lungs with every puff, eventually causing them to stiffen and lose their elasticity, destroying their ability to shrink down and blow air out. The delicate, grapelike cluster of tiny air sacs that make up the normal lung are eventually enlarged and destroyed by tobacco tars—again, an *irreversible* process that is the principal cause of emphysema. Emphysema slowly kills its victim by smothering him to death from lack of oxygen. A tiny bit of emphysematous change will begin in the lungs with the first cigarette, and continue in a progressive manner every year you smoke.

In 1914 there were 371 reported deaths from lung cancer in America. Today, thousands of Americans die from it every year. Lung cancer is the leading cause of all cancer deaths, with the vast majority (85 percent of them) caused by cigarette smoking. Lung cancers are particularly dangerous because very early in their development (usually before they are detected) they are prone to metastasizing—i.e., spreading throughout the bloodstream to other organs in the body. By the time they are found, they have usually spread from the lungs to the liver, brain, or bones.

Few smokers ever realize that with the discovery of the link between lung cancer and smoking, they've been given the option to eliminate a major threat to their life—an option that tens of thousands of cancer-ridden victims before them were, because of ignorance, denied. *That option is to quit smoking*. In other words, the key to treatment of lung cancer lies in prevention—and the most effective prevention is giving up smoking.

Looking on the bright side, no matter how long or how much you've smoked, when you *stop* smoking, the body starts regenerating. Some people find themselves coughing for days after they've quit smoking and are confused about it. Their lungs are simply trying to get rid of all the mucus and secretions that were produced when they smoked. The process of bodily repair is miraculous. It's been said that if the average smoker (again, the one who hasn't done too much damage) were examined by a physician five years after stopping, the physician would be unable to tell that the person ever smoked.

Sometimes the normality of things can be surprising. There are people who started smoking when they were 13 or 14 years old and quit when they were 46 years old. During almost their entire lives, they've been unable to taste or smell anything in its true flavor or fragrance. Long dulled by the effects of cigarettes, the senses soon readjust and come alive once again.

Many of those who quit smoking are impatient about the

results—they want to be rewarded for their efforts by dramatic changes in how they look and how they feel. The reward, however, is far more than just the pleasant, superficial changes. It is winning the chance to extend your own life span. By quitting smoking, you will have conquered a powerful addiction—probably the most serious, self-imposed threat that now exists to your own well-being. Think of the pride in your commitment and success in being able to overcome this disabling addiction.

The case against smoking is the case against *your* not smoking. You owe it to yourself to quit. For your health, first and foremost, but also for the rich and full enjoyment of your social life; for being accepted comfortably for the person you really are—free of a dangerous prop the media sold long ago when the risks were unknown, and continues to sell despite the tragic mortality rate. Free of being controlled by a powerful habit that impedes your chances for a long and healthy life.

2

Knowing Yourself Is Important

The Truth About Why You Smoke

In the many psychological studies done on the development of addictive habits, one of the things that has been discovered is that drug addicts and alcoholics have far more "logical" habits than cigarette smokers. When a drug addict or an alcoholic is looking for something to calm him down or make him feel better, he drinks a bottle of whiskey or sniffs cocaine. He might make himself pretty sick, and he may end up in a hospital or jail in the process, but at least he creates a momentary state of euphoria. With cigarettes, you are not going off into euphoric states; you are not calming down; you are not escaping anything. Quite the opposite is happening.

Most people who smoke believe that smoking calms them down. But these same people who claim they smoke to calm themselves down invariably claim they are always tense. If cigarettes did indeed calm them down, you'd think they'd be the calmest people in the world after twenty or thirty or forty cigarettes a day. However, we know it is not so.

A study was conducted at Harvard University of 3,000 cigarette smokers who claimed that they smoked cigarettes to calm themselves down when they became tense. The testing was conducted through winter, spring, summer, and fall, early in the morning, late at night, and in midafternoon, during stress periods and during relaxation periods. The conclusion was that regardless of the season, the time of day, or whether the person was nervous or relaxed, every one of the 3,000 participants increased their level of tension after each cigarette. *In no case did smoking relax anyone.*

Think again when you give yourself a million good reasons for smoking. Does it really satisfy any need? Does it truly relax you? Does it help you stay alert? Does it—as the "experts" theorize—meet a deep-seated need for oral fulfillment?

In fact, *none* of these explanations reveals the one basic, underlying truth of why you smoke:

You smoke because you are addicted to nicotine.

It's that simple. You are hooked on one of the most addictive drugs known to mankind, and you became addicted to it the day after you smoked your first cigarette.

The power of tobacco over the smoker cannot be underestimated. Experiments show that animals—chimpanzees and dogs, for example—become addicted to tobacco after inhaling as few as *four cigarettes*. In other words, after just four cigarettes, the nonsmoking chimpanzee is transformed into a confirmed addict, choosing cigarettes as a reward for certain behavior and even begging for more.

Nicotine is received through specialized cell formations located in the human brain and muscle tissues. These receptors have the capacity to recognize and react to nicotine when it is present in the body, signaling a wide range of physical reactions. Changes occur in heart rate, brain waves, and skin temperature; blood pressure rises and peripheral blood circulation slows; and hormones affecting the central nervous system are released.

In fact, it's the action on the brain and nervous system that helps create the body's dependence on nicotine. Many young to middle-aged people have been exposed to marijuana. They've given it a few tries, decided they didn't like it, and never touched it again. Given the same number of cigarettes, those same people would probably become addicted almost immediately. Even if it produces nausea at first, once the craving for tobacco begins, it continues relentlessly with every puff so that, in due course, the five-cigarette-a-day smoker becomes the ten-cigarette-a-day smoker (or more), and the struggle to quit becomes an increasing challenge. The craving does not aways cease with abstinence, either. There are people who stopped smoking thirty years ago, and *still* have a craving to smoke—which is why a program like ours, which works to block that craving, can be so effective over the long term.

Why did you *start* smoking? It wasn't for the taste, but rather because of something connected with the image and the media's promise that cigarettes would somehow improve your status or performance, whatever it might be. You were at a party and everyone else was smoking. Cigarettes gave you a kind of grown-up feeling. Smoking helped relieve the pressure of studying for exams and term papers. Whatever the original reasons, they have long gone by the boards, while the addiction has continued, as strong as ever. Thus, the adult smoker is merely a perpetuation of the adolescent smoker; the boy who smoked because he was nervous about school is now the adult who smokes because he's nervous about his job.

But imagine a society in which tobacco had never existed—no cigarettes, no cigars, no pipes. And one day, one of your trusted friends came to you and said he had a brilliant idea—one that would make you rich beyond your wildest dreams. Not opposed to being a multimillionaire, you asked this friend to explain his idea. And he told you he wanted to manufacture a little white paper cylinder about two to three inches long and stuff it with chopped, dried leaves. The people he would sell it to would put one end of the white cylinder into their mouths and set fire to the other end. They would then inhale a cloud of toxic smoke into their lungs and then blow the smoke out of their mouths and noses. Your friend insists that people would love it. They would do it all the time—thirty or forty cylinders a day, every day.

As he explained this "brilliant" idea to you, wouldn't you look at him as if he were crazy? Who in their right mind would set fire to something and willingly inhale toxic smoke into their lungs? So you ask him if there are any benefits—is it going to act as a tranquilizer or make the person more creative?—and he answers, no, it's just going to give them something to do.

If you've never thought about why you smoke quite this way before, this is what cigarettes really are, without the media image!

At the beginning of their addiction, many smokers felt not only that smoking was a harmless thing to do (after all, no ones dies of cancer from just three or four cigarettes), but also that they could quit whenever they wanted to. Unfortunately, most of them found that they could not quit at whim. Rather, their need for cigarettes increased—the casual smoker quickly becoming more heavily addicted. It may be a nonexistent threat in the beginning, but spread over a lifetime, it's that long-term addiction of the heavy smoker that ultimately causes the serious, smoking-related illnesses.

In tandem with the addiction, the whole performance cigarettes require becomes a conditioned response that makes it much harder to give up. We'll examine the performance aspect of smoking in chapter 3. For now, do not despair about your addiction. You are not a weak, terrible person with no will power. You are caught up in a powerful addiction to smoking. But powerful as it is, there is a way of getting out of it. Many, many thousands of people before you have overcome their smoking addiction with the method of hypnosis presented in this book—and so will you.

It's time to get over the idea that you are *hopelessly* addicted to cigarettes, because you are not. Imagine that there was no heart disease, no cancer, no emphysema, no shortness of breath, no pale skin or dulled senses connected with smoking. Imagine instead that every time you lit up a cigarette a big pimple would appear on the tip of your nose, or the outside of your chest would become blackened and sticky. How many people do you believe would smoke?

The truth is, as any doctor would tell you, people tend to dismiss the things they cannot see. But a major blemish on your face or body would demand immediate attention and throw your smoking addiction out the window—just as coughing up blood would galvanize you to quit. Only then, quitting might be too late.

Getting to know yourself—your true self—is important in laying the groundwork for this program. As for your ability to quit smoking . . . *You are probably not who you think you are*.

If I were to make a statement that you disagreed with, you'd probably tell me that you disagree with it. However, when you have your own thoughts about yourself, you don't disagree with them, or argue with yourself. They are part of your self-image and you don't question it. If you feel insecure about a situation, you accept that insecurity because it's part of your own unchallenged thought process. People who smoke assume they are not good at handling matters that require self-control. They convince themselves thay they cannot deal with their smoking habit. And they accept that as a reality. They do the same thing when they feel they're not a good public speaker, or that they're not going to be able to take this or that course.

What you think about yourself is not really a valid truth—but it's true to you because it's what you think about yourself. Smokers have a very clear image of who they are. They cannot see themselves drinking coffee without a cigarette; they cannot see themselves dealing with a meeting without cigarettes. They have constructed an individual in their brain who they believe to be their real self, but that person is just a figment of their imagination.

By changing your opinions about yourself, hypnosis introduces you to someone you never knew existed. A person who does, in fact, have the ability to stop smoking. A person who has the will power to be able to quit. Through hypnosis, you accept suggestions uncritically. If someone stated that they could take a knife and cut into your arm and you could watch them do this without pain, you would protest immediately. Your mind would tell you there's no way it could be done. But if you were hypnotized to the degree that would make this feat possible, you would accept the statement as a fact. Hypnosis, as anesthesia, has been used successfully in surgery for many years.

Hypnosis allows you to change long-held opinions and beliefs about yourself. It allows you to *believe* you are the kind of person who has the ability to stop smoking. *And you will*, because . . .

You can do what you believe you can do.

There is actually a correlation somewhere in the brain that tells you what you can do and what you cannot do. Can you, for example, jump up in the air six feet from a standing position? You say no. How do you know *no*? You know it because you've got an intelligence that tells you this cannot be done. On the other hand, you accept the fact that a trained athlete can do it. So can a human being do it? Yes. Can you do it? You respond with a *No*.

Until now, you may have believed that you cannot stop smoking. As explained above, this is based not on truth but your own perception. Just as hypnosis can help you change who you think you are, working on a subconscious level, it can also help you change what you think you can do. Hypnosis is the catalyst. It opens up that space—that willingness to try—that you need in order to shift gears and believe and expect that you can do something you had previously thought impossible.

There is a big difference between what you cannot do and what you will not do.

There are specific things that you truly cannot do, for whatever reason. For example, if someone offered you ten million dollars to lift an office building, you couldn't do it.

But what about the things you *will* not do, that you *can* do? "I will never give up cigarettes," you say, "because if I do, I'll die!" But if you were stuck in a room without any cigarettes, would you *really* die? No, you would not. Then is it theoretically possible that you can continue to live without smoking? Yes.

People confuse what they will not do with what they cannot do. "I can't stop smoking" is not true; "I *will not* stop smoking" is true. There's an acceptance in the subconscious mind about what one can do, and what one won't do. Would you speak before four thousand people at Carnegie Hall? I can't do that, you say. But that's not true. You *won't* do it—that's true. *Could* you do it? Yes. Badly, perhaps, but could you do it? Of course.

One has to separate I *cannot* from I *will not*. "I can't stop smoking" is such a final sentence that you blindly accept it. But it's not true. Having an addiction does not prevent you from thinking differently about yourself. Could you stop smoking if five million dollars were held in escrow, to be paid to you one year after quitting? And what if that pimple described earlier really *did* appear? Under certain conditions, you certainly *could* quit.

Motivation is half the battle, but you can also find clues of your own capability to quit. With smoking prohibited in so many places, these clues are more evident now than in the past. I know a rabbi who was a three-pack-a-day, four-pack-a-day smoker who could not stop smoking long enough to watch a Broadway show. Yet from Friday night, the beginning of the Sabbath, to Saturday night, when it was over, he never had any inclination to smoke a cigarette. It was as if they did not exist. The same holds true for the heavy smoker who won't sit in the smoking section at the back of a plane because it's too bumpy. She can go for three hours and never smoke a cigarette, only because she prefers to sit far forward. So the addiction isn't everything. And if it can be turned off for periods of time, it's certainly not impossible to quit smoking once and for all.

How to Make Reason Win Over Emotion

Smokers tells themselves they need to smoke during certain events or circumstances in their lives. "I smoke when I'm nervous," "I smoke when I'm under pressure at work," and so on. They depend on the "pleasure" of smoking to bolster their emotions.

As you prepare to quit smoking, but before you begin with hypnosis, you've got to make a very clear separation between your *emotions* and *reason*.

To understand how you're going to do this, think of smoking as if you were in a terribly attractive but doomed relationship—one which is filled with fire and romance, but also has fatal flaws. Let us say that one day you begin to assess the pros and cons of that relationship. You put the pluses—passionate love, exciting challenges, thrilling adventures—beside the minuses: already married, no interest in settling down or having a family, spends money frivolously, prefers play to work, and so forth. After looking at both sides of the picture, you could continue with the relationship, of course. But if those minuses outweigh the pluses, and you realize that nothing's going to change in the relationship, you are going to choose the reasonable path and break it off. "Yes, I still care very much about this person and it's going to be tough ending this relationship, but," you conclude, "if I'm ever going to move ahead with my life, I *must* break this thing off."

So you close off your mind and emotions to the relationship, and prepare to end it, knowing full well that no argument from yourself, or your ex-lover, is going to persuade you otherwise.

The process of closing your mind to smoking is the same as ending an emotionally charged relationship that's going nowhere. As in that relationship, having the desire to stop smoking has nothing to do with whether you enjoy it or not. Undoubtedly, you are giving up smoking *despite* the fact that you enjoy it. We would never make the assumption that people who come to our seminars to lose weight hate fattening foods. We rightly assume that they enjoy fattening foods. The fact that you're reading this book to quit smoking, and would enjoy a cigarette right now, has nothing to do with why you are stopping. You are quitting for yourself, for your health, for your future well-being and success.

Once again, the success of this program is based in part on the depth of your commitment to quit:

I will quit smoking and there will be no circumstances in which I will ever go back to smoking. There is no room for ever considering it again.

At the opening of this book, you signed the promise to yourself to quit. Now you must reinforce that commitment with reason.

Take a few moments to think of all the pleasures of smoking—the nice things tied to your emotions: it satisfies your cravings, puts you at ease, makes you comfortable—whatever else you find pleasurable. Put them on one side of a piece of paper, as if they were in a column in a ledger sheet. Next to it, in a separate column, list all the reasons why you should stop: for your health (and list specifics, such as being short of breath, if they are evident); for the good of your family; to improve your tennis game; because it is becoming more uncomfortable to smoke in many circumstances.

With these lists, you have separated reason from emotion. Now you've got to look at them calmly and in the comfort of your own home and decide to make a commitment, a value judgment, based on reason. Your commitment is that you are going to give up smoking. After this three-hour session, there will be no circumstances under which you will ever smoke again. That's your commitment. That's your logical, reasonable value judgment after seeing the facts. Every time an emotion challenges you to smoke, you will fall back on your logical commitment.

You've got to tell yourself: *There are no conditions under which I will ever smoke again.*

You've got to remind yourself: *You are not giving up smoking because it's not pleasurable.* You are giving up smoking because of the clear-cut reasons you have listed—reasons that have nothing to do with your emotions. No one can quit smoking on an emotional basis; you have to quit on a logical basis, after digesting the facts and then interpreting them—looking at the debits and the assets and making a decision. In this book, you'll never be expected to put up with terrible withdrawal symptoms.

Separating emotion from reason, you will stop smoking by following the program in this book. You have made the commitment to yourself to go through with it, and hypnosis will give you the will power to live up to that commitment.

3

It's Time to Finally Kick the Habit

The Evolution—and Undoing— of Your Smoking Habit

Smokers who are ready to quit are surprised when they discover that the same conditioning process that got them into their smoking habit can ultimately get them out of it.

How a habit starts. While your initial contact with cigarettes was almost immediately addictive, you had no *pattern* of smoking when you started. All you had was a pack of cigarettes and a feeling of nausea when you smoked them, but you smoked them anyway. Typically, if you started smoking as a teenager, you smoked when you could avoid your parents and their friends. Your pattern or habit of smoking evolved later on when you were able to arrange it around your life style.

A habit specifically implies doing something unconsciously and with premeditation; one's smoking habit is no exception. If you were to unobtrusively chart the actions of a person who seems to smoke twenty cigarettes randomly during the day, you'd find there is a definite pattern. His first cigarette is smoked within a certain number of minutes after he wakes up. That's always the same. And out of the total of twenty cigarettes, between waking up and evening, you'd find there's a slot time each of them is smoked that's accurate within one or two cigarettes every day.

The pattern is set through certain associations the smoker is no longer conscious of relating to—exactly as Pavlov found when he trained his dogs. Remember that experiment in psychology? Pavlov conditioned his canine subjects to salivate, as if getting food, every time a bell rang. He started by ringing a bell, waiting about five minutes, and then giving the dogs a piece of meat. He would repeat this simple exercise every day. In the beginning, whenever the dogs saw the meat, they began to salivate. By the end of the first week, Pavlov noticed that the dogs would anticipate the food and begin to salivate when they heard the bell ring. They were no longer just responding to the sight of the food—they had been conditioned to respond to the bell. Pavlov discovered that when he rang the bell, his dogs were ready to eat.

All human beings follow similar types of conditioned reflexes, smokers included. Smokers have conditioned themselves with many "bells," or associations, that trigger their automatic response to light up—pouring a cup of coffee in the morning; finishing a meal; getting into a car; hearing the telephone ring; starting to type at work; popping open a beer. A pack and a half a day gets smoked without even counting; the conditioned reflex is repeated hundreds of thousands of times.

When Pavlov was conducting his experiment, he called the ringing of the bell a stimulus, and the dogs salivating the response. With smoking, as will be explained later in this chapter, one of the wonderful things hypnosis can do is to come between the stimulus and the response. The stimulus may present itself—whether it's a cup of coffee, a telephone ringing, finishing a meal—but hypnosis creates a divider that prevents you from acting on the thought and responding to it by taking the cigarette. Moreover, you will not feel frustrated or deprived, because you are literally going to lose interest in smoking—and gain a wonderful sense of control over your habit.

Getting Your Daily Nicotine Dose

Unknown to themselves and to most observers, each smoker's own cigarette performance is orchestrated by a fixed amount of nicotine that has been established within the individual. As with eating food, you have programmed your body to take in a fixed amount of nicotine each day.

A typical approach to getting one's daily dose would begin in the morning with the first cigarette, thus sending a burst or "bolus" of nicotine to the brain that produces an almost immediate feeling of euphoria or satisfaction. For the rest of the day, the smoker tries to maintain this feeling by manipulating his or her intake of tobacco smoke—inhaling more or less deeply, taking more or fewer puffs, and smoking at different intervals.

When more than a certain number of cigarettes are smoked, acute toxic effects resembling nicotine overdose are experienced, such as nausea, lightheadedness, and a marked rise in heart rate. Some quitting programs try to force feed, or overdose their clients on cigarettes to the point of disgust. Smoking to distress can be instrumental as a prelude to a quit-smoking program, but alone, it is not going to be the means to quit. The problem with it is that while the person does become disgusted with cigarettes because of the addiction, the temporary revulsion doesn't last. This is easily demonstrated whenever the nicotine quota is surpassed. On New Year's Eve, for example, you may smoke 50 percent more cigarettes than usual because of being up five hours later than usual. (With scheduled events, some smokers will actually prepare to reprogram their smoking pattern by carrying an extra pack of cigarettes; they anticipate their increased need.) You'll finally become tired of smoking, but by the time you wake up the morning, you'll be ready to resume your normal smoking habit, whatever that might be.

When fewer than a minimum number of cigarettes is smoked, which appears for many people to be about ten cigarettes a day, satisfactory nicotine levels cannot be maintained and the smoker begins to experience distress. Years ago, when it became dangerous to smoke, most of the companies made filter cigarettes. And invariably, all the people who were smoking a pack of nonfiltered cigarettes a day, started to smoke a pack and a quarter of filter cigarettes a day. They needed to meet their quota of nicotine, and did so by smoking more cigarettes.

So in the mind somewhere, there is a series of conditions and conditioning that makes people accept the fact that (a) they are smokers, and (b) that they are smokers with a habit, under normal circumstances, equal to twenty or thirty or however many cigarettes a day, of a more or less specific brand, with a whole series of setups in their mind as to when they smoke—when they get up, go to the bathroom, have coffee, play cards. They may not know it, but all these things happen. What at first appears to be a casual, unordered routine, in short, turns out to be not casual at all, but a controlled behavior.

Once, while waiting for a friend to come out of a department store, I found myself observing a woman smoking a cigarette. She'd raise her hand to her mouth, take a puff, lower her hand, wait a bit, and take another puff. The gestures involved were so automatic that, for want of something to do, I timed them with my watch—twenty seconds *exactly* between each puff.

Dependence of the Mind—
or Only of the Body?

Although the general acceptance of nicotine and tobacco is as an addictive drug, (remember the rabbi in chapter 2), curious things can happen to show that *the mind set is often stronger than the addiction.*

I had a friend, a lawyer, who was in fact one of the most chronically addicted smokers I've ever known. He would smoke three packs a day, nonstop. Some years ago, when we were both in London on business, we took the opportunity to visit a tailor in Savile Row, and my friend bought himself a very, very expensive suit. Because we had to come back before the tailoring was finished, the suit was shipped to the States and my friend wore it for the first time to a cocktail party—a charity event at the Plaza Hotel in New York that both of us were invited to attend. As we drove together to this engagement, chatting in the car, an ash from his cigarette flew back through the window and landed on his jacket. We didn't discover it until we smelled burning, and it had burned a hole—not just a hole, but a large area—through the jacket and part of his pants. He took the cigarettes, crumbled them up, threw them out the window, and never, ever smoked again.

So although the smoker may accept cigarettes as addictive, there *is* a second state of the mind present that can shift the dependency from one stage to another and eventually allow it to stop. My friend's case, much like the smoker who quits when a friend dies of lung cancer, is one of those unusual, spur-of-the-moment shifts to the extreme. But smokers are readjusting their smoking habits all the time to suit their needs, or rules.

Many, many people choose to give up smoking during Lent or other religious times. This is quite impossible with a drug like heroin, which involves a horrendous physical dependency—you couldn't make a mental choice between turning it off and turning it on. Other smokers have trained themselves, because of all the nonsmoking rules that have been established in public places, to temporarily readjust their normal pattern of habit—let's say, a cigarette every twenty to twenty-five minutes—to something more sporadic. The adjustment can even be handled when the changes in one's smoking pattern are more long-range. For example, if you always worked in an office where you could smoke, and now you're starting a new job in an office where you cannot smoke, there may be a kind of temporary confusion because suddenly you are aware that at a certain time something is supposed to be happening that isn't. But the mind is quick to reassemble what's familiar, and after a while, it provides a new pattern for your smoking. Now you're going to smoke in the bathroom; before, you never did. Or in the building lobby. The new pattern soon becomes as automatic as the old one. For if your previous pattern, or habit, was thirty cigarettes a day, somehow you are going to get in thirty cigarettes a day on this job, too. You will take your dosage of the day, even though the circumstances have changed.

At the onset of our program, when a person who has all of his patterns preset is told she's going to stop smoking in three hours, she doesn't understand what that means, or how it's going to happen. However, in hypnosis the individual accepts suggestions uncritically—thus even the incomprehensible suggestion that she will quit the habit becomes possible.

Before we had perfected our stop-smoking program at the Institute of Hypnotherapy, and it went on for several sessions instead of just one, we found that clients coming in weren't sure *when* they were supposed to stop smoking. They would say when they left one session, "Well, am I supposed to stop between now and the next session, or what?" All that changes when we decided that if the client were coming to a smoking session on June 16th, then he or she would come prepared to quit on the 16th. They'd anticipate the cut-off date, and suddenly, everything became easier.

If the addiction can be adjusted, it can be turned off for good. The person who smokes does not believe he can stop. He does not believe he is capable of stopping. He's not even sure he can stop for a couple of hours. Again, that's a mind set. It isn't true. It's also easy to dismiss the idea of quitting because it's too ingrained a habit. The smoker will say, "I've had this smoking habit for fifty years. I can't break it." Of course she doesn't *want* to give up a habit or a conditioning because it satisfies something in her. And she would rather convince herself she'll be worse off for quitting. So she tells herself, "I don't know whether I'll get sick from smoking or not—all I do know is that if I quit smoking, I'll become a raving maniac in two days." And this she accepts as gospel truth. But what about the people who quit smoking without any withdrawal symptoms or any weight gain? Each smoker simply fulfilled his or her own expectations.

Which of these mind **sets**, then, would *you* choose?

The fact that hundreds of thousands of people have stopped smoking—the fact that other people have stopped for various reasons—makes it a positive thing. It would be very difficult to think, "Well, no one has ever done this before." But millions of people *have*. Yes, quitting smoking is tough, but you know something? It's not as tough as you think it is.

Breaking the Habit of Smoking

Here's where we come back to the conditioned response—and Pavlov's Dogs—as the key to quitting.

The smoker mistakenly believes that *to think about a cigarette is to smoke it*. He's oblivious of the fact that—as with every other conditioned response that has to do with an addiction—smoking a cigarette involves three wholly separate elements:

1. *The stimulus*—e.g., a phone call, having coffee, stress
2. *The response*—taking the cigarette
3. *The reinforcement*—smoking the cigarette

First, the *stimulus* to smoke has to be triggered in you, either consciously or subconsciously. You walk into a room and smell cigarette smoke. You may be aware of smelling it or you may not, but somehow it produces a desire to smoke. Or you see a cigarette ad, or someone offers you a cigarette. Just because you have that desire or thought, however, doesn't mean you have to smoke. You haven't taken the cigarette, you've just had the desire for it.

So the next stop, then, involves action: the response of taking the cigarette into your hand. But again, simply holding a cigarette in your hand does not mean that you have to fill your lungs with smoke.

You need to reinforce the response—lighting up the cigarette and smoking it—reinforcing the desire.

These three elements, whether they are applied to eating, drinking, smoking, or any other addiction, always come into play: The thought, the action, and the reinforcement.

Hypnosis is able to create an interference between the stimulus and the response. The thought of smoking comes to mind, but the person does not act on it. Therefore a new response—abstaining from smoking—is reinforced.

No one can stop the initial thought. But thoughts cost *nothing*. Thoughts do not cause you to cough or put your health and life at serious risk. There are pople who have stopped smoking (or stopped drinking) years ago who, even today, find that the thought comes into their mind of taking a drink or smoking a cigarette, but they don't act on it.

They don't go beyond their desire. Some people carry cigarettes they do not smoke. I believe they are foolishly tempting fate, but if they hold on to them yet don't smoke them, they're still breaking the cycle of their addiction.

Habits can be broken if the habit can be broken into segments, and then each segment looked at independently. The habit is not smoking the cigarette; that's the final conclusion.

So think again if you have accepted your smoking as a fait accompli: that is, to want a cigarette is to smoke it. As with every habit, there are formats involved prior to doing it, and wanting the cigarette is only one part of it. To complete the cycle, you've got to take the cigarette, light it, lift it up to your mouth, and smoke it—each a very separate, subconscious movement that, through hypnosis, can also be dealt with on a subconscious level. During hypnosis, the will to quit sinks in so deeply it subconsciously arrests your actions to smoke—thereby interfering with the response, and thus breaking your smoking habit.

4

Preparing to Stop Smoking Forever

As you'll recall, my lawyer friend, the three-pack-a-day smoker described in chapter 3, crumpled up his cigarettes in a rage when he burned the hole in his beautiful new suit, and never smoked again. Whether quitting is spur-of-the-moment (as it was for my friend) or carefully planned (as it is for the majority of people), smokers who *close their minds to the possibility of ever smoking again* are the ones who succeed at it.

Conversely, without getting the "mind set" in place, the smoker who attempts to quit is not likely to be successful.

Let me explain the "mind set" more clearly.

There is an interesting thing about what the subconscious accepts, and what it won't ever consider. Let's say your house is worth half a million dollars and a potential buyer says to you, "I'm looking for a house and I understand yours is for sale. I'd like to offer you the best price I can. I can offer you $50,000."

Now, something happens when you hear an offer of $50,000 on your house that is worth half a million dollars. Your mind isn't even willing to consider any further conversation. There's no point discussing it. Very different, I might add, from the potential buyer who says to you, "Look, you may or may not get your price, but I can offer you $425,000. Why don't you think it over, talk it over with your spouse, and let me know." You may not accept the offer, but your mind at least may be open to it.

To succeed at quitting smoking, the first thing you've got to do is get the proper mind set to do so. In chapter 2, you listed the pluses and minuses of smoking, side by side, as on a ledger sheet. With that list in hand, you can certainly continue to smoke, if that's your choice. Nobody is going to stop you. If you decide you want to stop because of the liabilities, you have to go the next step beyond *wanting* to quit to making the commitment to quit—a commitment that has with it no leeway, no opening, no possibilities for ever smoking again. You've got to say to yourself: *"I will quit smoking, and under no conditions will I ever go back to smoking."* Ever.

Then you have got to close your mind to the idea of ever smoking again.

You have made your commitment in writing, on page 6. Now you are ready to prepare to be a successful nonsmoker.

From years of experience, we have seen that *preparing* to quit is a fundamental strategy to the success of the program. Your subconscious mind needs tangible signs to convince it that preliminary actions toward quitting are already underway. To do that, you've got to assume the role of a nonsmoker. Right here and now. Because after the next phase of the program, where you will be using self-hypnosis, you will *become* a nonsmoker.

The following 8-point nonsmoker strategy outlined here is ready and waiting for you to put to good use after this three-hour session. It reveals the success secrets of those who have quit. Here's how they did it:

1. *Successful quitters get rid of the evidence.*

You've made your personal commitment to quit. Now go through your home, office, briefcase, purse, bureau drawers, etc., and get rid of the ashtrays, matches, cigarette lighters—all the paraphernalia connected with smoking. Give it away, throw it away, donate it to the thrift shop—permanently remove it from your life.

Remove the smell of smoke from your clothes and environment. Empty your closet and take your wardrobe to the cleaners. Schedule a thorough housecleaning that will remove the residue of smoke from drapes, carpets, and upholstery. Open the windows and air out the rooms.

If there are other smoking members of your family who cannot be convinced to quit with you, proceed ahead with the housecleaning, getting rid of your own smoking paraphernalia. You will still experience the real and tangible sense of change connected with these activities. Besides, your commitment to quit is to yourself (see 6 below), and it does not include the possibility of being defeated by those smoking around you.

Note: If you find yourself hesitant about permanently getting rid of the evidence, you don't trust yourself to remain a nonsmoker. Go back and reevaluate your commitment to quit. Get your mind set more firmly in place. You cannot proceed, otherwise.

2. *Successful quitters tell all the world.*

They have such confidence in their personal commitment to quit that they make it public.

Go ahead and tell all your friends, family, and co-workers that you are quitting smoking. That you *have* quit. *Bore* them with it! "Going public" is the strongest psychological ploy for living up to your commitment to quit.

Note: If you hear yourself saying, "But I don't want to tell anyone I'm quitting smoking," it means that deep down you are thinking, "If I fail, I'll feel like a fool." But there's no room for failure in your commitment, remember? Go back and get it more firmly in place. And begin the self-confidence exercise at the end of this chapter.

3. *Successful quitters quit all at once.*

They accept the proven fact that *cutting down is not the answer.*

Of the people you know who have quit smoking (family, friends, et cetera), has anyone succeeded by cutting down? The odds are that they have not. In all of the tests, experiments, and scientific evaluations, cutting down has been shown to be the worst possible way of quitting smoking, with a very poor likelihood of success. Prepare to be a nonsmoker by preparing to quit all at once.

Note: If you say to yourself, "But it's impossible for me to quit cold turkey. I've been smoking too much for too long to do it that way," then you have not closed your mind to smoking. If you cut down gradually, you'll almost surely fail; and you are tempting yourself to accept the idea that you'll never make it! Stop reading and reevaluate the degree of your commitment to quit.

4. *Successful quitters quit on a specific day.*

For you, that day is set. You set it when you bought this book.

Those who come to our Quit-Smoking Seminars know in advance that the day of the session is the day that they will quit. They come in prepared to quit—just as you are now preparing to quit before moving on to the self-hypnosis exercises in chapters 6 and 7.

Note: If you find yourself having trouble picking a day to quit, or are postponing it because you are "waiting for a calm time in your life," you will never quit. *No* time is a calm time!

5. *Successful quitters think and act like nonsmokers.*

They assume the role of a nonsmoker—a person who has absolutely no use for cigarettes at all.

You've got to visualize yourself as a nonsmoker and act like one, right now. That means you cannot allow the thought to come into your mind that you are willing to recontemplate the idea of smoking. And if that thought comes to your mind, you have to refuse to discuss it with yourself, just as you would if you were tempted to rekindle the romantic but destructive relationship. In the same way that your mind clicked off when you heard a $50,000 offer on your $500,000 house, there is no room for discussion about smoking, and you just don't think about it. You are a nonsmoker now. A nonsmoker does not carry cigarettes. A nonsmoker does not contemplate whether or not he has enough cigarettes to get through until tomorrow. A nonsmoker does not orchestrate the pattern and flow of his day around when or where he can smoke a cigarette. A nonsmoker has no association of any description with cigarettes.

Earlier, you read about arguing with yourself, or talking to yourself. You have much more control over your mind than you think you have. If the thought ever begins to come into your mind concerning your previous life as a smoker, a life that no longer exists, you have the power to cut it off by assuming the role of a nonsmoker. That idea is simply not for you.

Note: If you balk at picturing the idea of being a nonsmoker, and all that it entails, before you quit, your commitment may still be on shaky ground. By putting yourself in the nonsmoker's shoes now, acting a part that is void of emotions about cigarettes, you add a shield of protection around your commitment to quit.

6. *Successful quitters quit for themselves, for the glory of their personal success.*

Occasionally, people come to our quit-smoking seminars and explain that they are stopping for somebody else. That someone else in their life has been pressuring them to do this. Even if someone wants you to do this, it is very important that you accept the reality that you are quitting for yourself. If you stop "for someone else," the tendency is to do one of two things. Either you immediately walk out of the session, get into a fight with that person, and say, "Well, now look what you made me do. Everything was fine before I tried to stop smoking." Or you stop smoking and every day make that person's life more miserable, knowing that somewhere down the line, they're going to look at you and say, "That's it. Take the damn cigarette." And you'll say, "Okay. You know how hard I tried," knowing you've been setting this up from Day One.

True motivation to quit comes from within. It comes from the notion of triumphing, or basking in the glory of one's personal success—standing proud and tall in the ranks of the millions of men and women who have battled their addiction and made it through to quitting cigarettes forever. Successful quitters are the ones who recognize their quitting as the difference between failure and success. They feel it on a visceral level. If you fail at this, it's going to be a personal failure because the only person who can stop you from smoking is yourself. If you're going to be successful, then the motivation lies in the appreciation of your own success. You can bask in the glory of it, feeling good about yourself and triumphant in the company of your family and friends, for the rest of your life.

Note: If you find yourself quitting for someone else, or quitting for some other reason than for your own personal glory, health, and success, stop and review your personal commitment. Get the reasons behind it fixed more clearly in place.

7. *Successful quitters prepare to quit by building self-confidence.*

Over and over we see that when an atheleate sets a new record, his competitors quickly try to match or even better it. We see women athletes training for competition, and moving closer to the ranks of their male counterparts, where once it was unheard of that they compete at all. Before attempting "the impossible," the mind needs proof that something can be done. With smoking, that proof lies in statistics. To date, there are twenty-seven million adults who smoke, but there were over forty million in 1964 when the Surgeon General's report first appeared. You can continue with this quit-smoking program with every confidence that people just like you have succeeded with it—chronic smokers, heavy smokers, hardcore smokers. Following the method in this book, you can proceed toward your goal with the confidence of knowing that you are in the hands of the world's leading experts on quitting smoking. We have had to find a solution for hundreds of thousands of chronic smokers. There are plenty of books written on the subject today that are based not on practical knowledge, but rather on theory alone. That is not the case with us. We offer a refund to anyone who attends our quit-smoking seminar and is not completely satisfied with his response, and we'd be out of business if the program didn't work. Instead, we've thrived. Word-of-mouth recommendations from those who have participated in our Quit-Smoking Program have kept us busy for thirty years. We receive constant, positive feedback because our program, as presented here in this book, really works.

"I wish I had come to you twenty years ago to quit."

"I smoked two packs a day for the last ten years and now I don't even think of cigarettes. Thank you for helping me quit so painlessly."

"I knew I could do it, but I never knew it would work for my husband. I'm amazed!"

These are but some of the actual responses we have gotten from participants filling out our questionnaires in the weeks after attending a Petrie Quit-Smoking Session. With these people, and the thousands of others who've followed the program in this book, you couldn't have picked a better time than now to quit smoking.

8. *Successful quitters quit on a day-by-day basis.*

They don't worry about how they are going to do in the future; they're confident about how they'll do right now.

We live in a society where people spend so much time feeling discouraged about past failures, or worrying about something that's going to happen in the future, that it is easy to lose sight of the fact that—as with any other habit—you've got to learn to deal with quitting *in the present*. But you've got to be absolute. And that means you don't go into situations saying to yourself, "Okay, let's see how I'm going to do." You go into situations saying to yourself, "I don't give a damn what happens; I am not taking a cigarette." You are determined and committed to succeeding, not *hoping* to do well. Having *hope* is nice, but it's no way to convince your subconscious that you are really going to quit smoking. Insomniacs experience a classic example of what is referred to as "Hope Psychology." Some people have trouble sleeping one night, lie down in bed the next night, and say to themselves, "I'm so tired, I'm going to sleep like a log." And they do. Others have trouble sleeping one night, lie down the next night, and say, "I'm so tired. I couldn't sleep last night. I *sure hope* I can fall asleep tonight." When you use the word *hope*, is it success that you're implying? No, it's failure. You are not going to walk away from this program thinking, I hope this works. You are going to put the book down after the program is over, determined and committed to making it work. It's your life. Your health. And it's probably one of the most positive, and healthiest, things you've ever done for yourself.

5

How to Stop Smoking Without Gaining Weight

"Will I gain weight if I stop smoking?"

This is the question asked most often by smokers requesting information about the Petrie Method programs; for many would-be quitters, it's the all-important question that leaves their decision to quit hanging in the balance. At least when they ask, we can give them facts—and relieve them from their worries about weight gain. One third of all smokers, however, don't even think to ask the question. For them, the fear of putting on weight is so real that they would never even *dare* to consider quitting. "My sister-in-law quit smoking and gained thirty pounds. I'd kill myself first," they say, oblivious of falling into a faulty logic trap—i.e., of concluding that what happens to some people happens to all people. It doesn't have to happen that way. The pregnant woman who listens to her friend describe how she was immobilized by morning sickness mistakenly concludes that *all* pregnant women are immobilized by morning sickness in the early months of their pregnancy—and is then surprised when she doesn't have a single bout of it.

This kind of thinking prevails in many areas where there is anxiety or apprehension. Sorting out fact from fallacy, however, confirms that weight gain is *not* an unavoidable consequence of stopping smoking:

FACT: Not everyone gains weight when they quit

smoking. Some people gain, some lose, and some remain the same weight as before they quit. *It all depends on the individual.*

While some people do gain weight after they quit smoking—for reasons explained further in this chapter—there are others who actually *lose* weight when they quit. Why don't we hear much about them? Because, again, what usually sinks in are the horror stories that reinforce our fears. For those individuals who worry about gaining weight, there are easy solutions later in this chapter for preventing this from happening.

FACT: You don't have to exchange smoking for eating when you give up cigarettes.

Another fallacy is the belief that when you give up one habit, you substitute or replace it with a secondary habit. You've got to trace the source of this belief back to its roots, and then see how ludicrous it is to apply it to the idea of replacing smoking with negative eating habits. The replacement theory originated through the observation of psychotics. Psychotics were put behind closed doors, forced to give up certain habits, and then exhibited secondary habits. Are smokers psychotics? Of course not. Readers of this book have been thinking about quitting, and have now decided for themselves that they are ready to do it.

Besides, it is the habit of your smoking—the pattern—and not the need for food that's behind the inclination to eat. If you smoke twenty to thirty cigarettes a day, taking five to ten drags on a cigarette, that adds up to somewhere between one hundred to three hundred times a day you have unthinkingly put something into your mouth. Not in your stomach—in your mouth. The problem comes when the person who stops smoking spends all day unthinkingly putting food *through* his mouth and into his stomach. Imagine how much weight you could gain if you had eaten something every time you had smoked a cigarette!

You don't have to fall into this trap when you stop smoking. If you are one of the ones who feels a temporary confusion when you quit—what to do with your hands and mouth that doesn't involve reaching out for food—there's a simple, easy solution for you. Get a stirrer from a cup of coffee, or one of those little plastic cigarettes, or a piece of carrot or celery. Hold a pencil between your teeth and toy with it while you work at your desk. Any of these things will provide a satisfactory substitute for the hand-to-mouth activity you're used to, without causing you to put on a pound. In time, you won't need them.

FACT: Metabolic changes that might occur in connection to quitting smoking are only temporary.

Not everyone experiences a change in his metabolism— i.e., the rate at which he burns fat—but it can happen in the early weeks after quitting smoking. Even if you are unaffected, you should understand what this means and be ready to make the slight adjustments in your diet to accommodate such changes. *They are only temporary.*

If you've ever heard someone who stopped smoking swear he is not eating any more but finds he's putting on weight, it is probably due to the fact that his metabolism has slowed down; his body no longer requires the same amount of food as it did before quitting. This situation will balance out as soon as the metabolism *returns* to its normal rate— that is, the rate of metabolism before you ever smoked. You have to understand that it is *smoking* that caused the metabolic change in the first place—unnaturally accelerating the metabolic process. After quitting, the body begins to calm down and relax, slowly returning to normal as the poisonous effects of nicotine leave the system. As with all the other systems, the metabolic process also returns to normal.

FACT: There's no need for special diets or special recipes to keep your post-smoking weight down. The trick is cutting down on carbohydrates.

As your body slowly returns to its normal metabolic rate, you can safely and confidently keep your weight on an even keel *without gaining an ounce*, if you cut back on your intake of foods made with flour and/or added sugar. The highest problem with metabolism is in the area of carbohydrates. Breads and other baked goods are a primary example of the type of food in this category to avoid, but the list at the end of this chapter will give you more specific guidelines.

By cutting carbohydrates out of your diet for two or three weeks after you've quit smoking, your metabolism will return to normal and you'll never gain an ounce in the process. Hypnosis will work with you to reinforce this objective.

FACT: An increase in hunger after quitting smoking is also a *temporary* situation.

As with changes in metabolism, some people experience a change in their appetite after they quit. They're the ones who, when they smoked, could go from seven in the morning to three in the afternoon with just cigarettes and coffee. Smoking diminished their appetites and now, without cigarettes, they find they are hungrier more often than before.

If you should experience this hunger, remember first of all that it's a temporary situation. You can help the body adjust back to normal—without gaining a pound—if you take notice of *how* you eat your food.

It's so simple, but it makes such sense: *Eat Slowly*. You have what is called an "appestat"—a built-in gauge that regulates the amount of food you eat, much the way a thermostat regulates the degree or level of heat in a house. This food gauge has to do with your blood sugar level. As you eat, your blood sugar level goes up, until it reaches a point where it triggers a sensation of fullness. That point is reached twenty to thirty minutes into eating, regardless of how much you eat. You can test this built-in, set point the next time you go out to a restaurant where food is served in courses. First comes the salad, or appetizer, which you eat with a little bread and butter. The waiter leaves you alone for fifteen to twenty minutes, and by the time the main course arrives, your hunger has already been satisfied.

When food isn't paced—in other words, when a meal is put in front of you all at once, and you are left to your own hungry devices to barrel through it—you can quickly eat three times more food before feeling full than you would if you ate only one portion slowly. Regardless of how hungry you feel when you've stopped smoking, you've *got* to pace yourself to eat slowly and in small amounts until your body has returned to its normal, nonsmoking state (a process that takes about 45 days) and you can get a more accurate picture of how much you require to maintain your correct weight.

By eating slowly, you give the body a chance to tell you if it needs less food. Give yourself small portions, and put the fork down until you finish what's in your mouth. Take the time to enjoy what you're eating—to delight in the pleasure of being able to really taste and smell your food; in other words, to rediscover the lost art of dining. And don't feel obligated to clean your plate, regardless of what your mother might have told you. If you find yourself satisfied after half or three-quarters of the meal, that's the point where you stop eating.

FACT: Some people stop smoking and lose weight simultaneously.

If you are inclined to try to meet this dual objective, you'll need to plan ahead and concentrate on a high protein, low carbohydrate, low fat diet. You must limit carbohydrate-heavy foods (including those listed at the end of the chapter) and you must select balanced, diversified foods. The kind of diet you would need is only temporary, and it's a diet your doctor should help you plan.

FACT: Vitamins can benefit the body in two ways after quitting: assisting the general recovery process, and replenishing those elements depleted by smoking.

Nobody knows the degree of disruption smoking causes to the main systems of the body, but one thing is certain: if you've smoked for ten years or twenty-five years, your body is a smoker's body, and it has had to make critical adjustments to prevent you from dying. The sudden absence of all those poisons (over two hundred of them, at last count) introduced to your system on a continual basis creates a temporary mix-up as the body shifts gear into recovery. Vitamins at this time will aid that recovery. The kinds of physical changes you might anticipate in the days immediately after you quit run the gamut from virtually nothing to certain quirky after-effects such as stomach aches, gas, or exhaustion. "Every knock is a boost," as they say. You can consider all of these as signs of avid recovery.

The body's vitamin supply is also thrown off balance as it adjusts to the new, nonsmoking you.

It's known that an excessive amount of vitamins are used when you smoke; that, for example, five or six cigarettes can deplete all the vitamin C in your body. In working with addictions, we have found that the use of vitamins on a regular basis when people change their diet or intake of food, or have quit smoking, helps balance out the body's needs and gives it a chance, then, to readjust to its new conditions.

Ask your doctor to recommend vitamins that would be

suitable at this time. Any vitamin from a leading pharmaceutical company is adequate, particularly those with a good portion of vitamin C.

If you are one of those people who hesitates to quit smoking because of how it might affect your weight, this chapter should put your fears to rest once and for all. You needn't gain a pound after you quit if you implement the threefold strategy outlined here:

1. Temporarily use nonfood substitutes for the hand-to-mouth habit
2. Temporarily cut back on carbohydrates
3. Eat slowly for the rest of your life

Expect some of the withdrawal symptoms described on page 123. Fortunately, once they wear off and your body regains its nonsmoking equilibrium, you are going to look and feel better than ever before. You won't need to pay special attention to your weight, provided you eat nourishing, balanced foods. Keeping excess pounds off is but one element in the life-extending process of repair and recovery that rewards you after you give up your smoking addiction. As described in chapter 1, the serious damage of smoking takes place within, where it can't be seen. This is also the place where the repair takes place. You have the incredible ability to stop the damage done by smoking now, before it is irreversible. Every cell in your body (with the exception of brain cells) regenerates every seven years. That means that seven years from now, there will be no trace of the "garbage" from cigarettes left in your system. Most of the cleanup actually takes place in the first year—a change process which, when you think of it being so soon within reach of those who quit, is no less than a miracle.

General Dietary Guidelines for First 45 Days After You Quit Smoking

Note: Skim The Dietary Guidelines and Stop-Smoking Eating Plan (pages 56–64) now, and go back to them after your three-hour session is over.

Salt

For health reasons, and because an excessive intake of salt may increase the retention of water in your body, you should not consume more than 3 to 8 grams of salt a day (1 teaspoon = 5 grams). Most people use 2 to 4 teaspoons a day, or an average of 15 pounds of salt a year!

The highest salt values occur in:

- Smoked, processed, or cured meats and fish, such as ham, bacon, corned beef, cold cuts, frankfurters, sausages, tongue, salt pork, chipped beef, anchovies
- Meat extracts, bouillon cubes, meat sauces
- Salted foods such as potato chips, nuts, popcorn, et cetera
- Condiments such as relishes, Worcestershire sauce, catsup, pickles, mustard, and olives
- Vegetable salts, as in onion, garlic, celery, parsley, et cetera
- Sodium ingredients, as contained in sodium benzoate (used as a preservative), monosodium glutamate (used as a flavoring aid), sodium hydroxide (used in food processing)
- Most bakery products
- Frozen fish
- Prepared flours, flour mixes, baking powder, baking soda
- Frozen peas and lima beans

- Canned meats, vegetables, fish, and fruit
- Sauerkraut, butter, cheese, and peanut butter

To season your food with little or no salt, use bay leaf, dry mustard powder, green pepper, marjoram, fresh mushrooms, nutmeg, onion, pepper, sage, thyme, lemon juice, paprika, parsley, poultry seasoning, curry powder, garlic, mint, mint jelly, pineapple, rosemary, apple, applesauce, apricot, ginger, oregano, vinegar, pimiento, fresh tomato, chives, dill, mace, saffron, brown sugar, cinnamon, basil, peppercorns.

Note: Generally, foods that are natural (unprocessed), such as meat, fish, poultry, cheese, salads, vegetables and fruits, have low sodium.

Sugar

Sugar is no more fattening than any other kind of food, but sugar has high-density calories. Some examples: You can consume more than a thousand calories on a dish of ice cream, a candy bar, and a wedge of pie. Some cereals contain between 40 percent and 50 percent sugar. A chocolate bar could have 7 teaspoons of sugar per ounce. A small wedge of chocolate cake can have as many as 15 teaspoons of sugar, and a wedge of cherry pie, 14 teaspoons of sugar. Twelve ounces of sweetened soda contains 9 to 12 teaspoons of sugar, and 8 ounces of Kool Aid contains 6 teaspoons of sugar.

General rule: Do not eat or drink a food if sugar has been added.

Water

Your body is about two-thirds water. Every living cell in your body depends on water. If you were to lose 5 percent of your body water, you would become ill. Lose 15 percent and it could be fatal.

In order to stop smoking healthfully, you should drink six to eight glasses of liquids a day, most of it in the form of water. Other liquids could include juice, low calorie sodas, or milk.

Exercise

Exercise is important because it ultimately affects the amount of calories you can eat. Eventually, the correlation between the two dictates whether you are fat or thin.

Not only does exercise force your body to burn more fat, it also causes your basal metabolic rate to stay higher for hours afterwards, promoting weight loss. You can actually estimate the additional weight loss that could occur in one year using one half hour per day at the listed activities:

Yearly Weight Loss in Pounds	Activity for ½ Hour a Day
14.07	Walking slowly
20.33	Golf, using power cart
28.15	Walking, 3 mph
28.15	Cycling slowly
28.15	Bowling
34.41	Tennis, doubles
34.41	Dancing
34.41	Golf, carrying clubs
34.41	Simple calisthenics
34.41	Walking 3.5 mph
40.67	Walking 4 mph
40.67	Cycling 10 mph
40.67	Ice skating
40.67	Roller skating
46.93	Tennis, singles
46.93	Folk dancing

46.93	Walking 5 mph
56.31	Jogging 5 mph
56.31	Paddleball
56.31	Basketball
56.31	Cycling 12 mph
56.31	Skiing

The Petrie Stop-Smoking Eating Plan

As further insurance that you will not gain weight after you stop smoking, you can follow the eating plan laid out here. You will see it is not really a diet, but rather an approach to food that makes perfect sense when the goal is establishing good, weight-conscious eating habits, especially when you quit smoking and your metabolism is adjusting to the change in your body.

Can you have a sandwich? Yes! Can you have a beer? Yes! Can you have salad dressing? Yes! Can you have pasta? Yes! Can you eat foods that are not included in this diet? No! (At least, not until you have passed the 45-day period after you quit smoking. Then, make comparable substitutes.)

How to Use the Eating Plan

The eating plan is made up of certain categories of "allowable" daily foods:

Three portions of vegetables
Three portions of fruit
Three portions of starches
Six portions of protein
Two portions of milk
Two portions of fats
Free foods

If you look at the table of foods under "starches," you will find that five ounces of beer is considered one portion. As you are allowed three portions of starch a day, you may decide to drink your starches by drinking 15 ounces of beer. Obviously, you should not do that. Similarly, if you look under "protein," you will see that you can have six portions. This could mean you could eat six eggs a day. Do not do that, either. Try to eat a sensible mix of foods in each category. Eat them in any combination you wish. For example, you can have one slice of toast (starch list), two eggs (protein list), and two slices of bacon (fat list) for breakfast.

You could make pepper steak with four ounces of lean beef (protein list), one teaspoon of oil (fat list), green peppers, and mushrooms (vegetable list), crushed thyme (free list), and grated Parmesan cheese (protein list).

You can bake, broil, fry, grill—in fact, you can prepare foods any way you wish. There are endless combinations of foods and menus that could be arranged.

If you take the time to think about your eating plan, you will find the time well spent in the days right after you quit smoking, and beyond.

FREE FOODS

Bouillon	Chicory	Chinese Cabbage	Clear soups
Coffee	Endive	Escarole	Gelatin; unsweetened
Lemon, Lime	Lettuce	Low Cal Sodas	Mustard, Herbs
Parsley	Pickles	Radishes	Tea
Soy Sauce	Vinegar	Watercress	Fresh Garlic

VEGETABLES: 3 PORTIONS DAILY
An Average Portion is 1/2 Cup Cooked or 1 Cup Raw.

Asparagus	Beets	Bean Sprouts	Beans, green or wax
Broccoli	Cabbage	Brussels Sprouts	Carrots
Celery	Cucumber	Cauliflower	Catsup (2 Tbsp)
Eggplant	Mushrooms	Okra	Onions
Peppers	Rutabaga	Sauerkraut	Summer Squash
Tomatoes	Veg. Juice	Tomato Juice	

FRUITS: 3 PORTIONS DAILY

Apple	1/2 Med.	Grape Juice	1/4 Cup
Apple Juice	1/3 Cup	Honeydew	1/3 Med.
Apple Sauce	1/2 Cup	Mango	1/2 Small
Apricots	2 Med.	Nectarine	1 Small
Apricots, dried	4 Halves	Orange Juice	1/2 Cup
Bananas	1/2 Small	Orange	1 Small
Blueberries	1/2 Cup	Papaya	1/3 Med.
Cantaloupe	1/4 Med.	Peach	1 Med.
Cherries	10 Large	Pear	1 Small
Dates	2	Pineapple	1/2 Cup
Figs, dried	1 Small	Pineapple Juice	1/3 Cup
Fruit Cocktail	1/2 Cup	Prunes, dried	2
Grapefuit Juice	1/2 Cup	Strawberries	3/4 Cup
Grapefruit	1/2 Small	Tangerine	1 Large
Grapes	12	Watermelon	1 Cup

STARCHES: 3 PORTIONS DAILY

BREADS:		CRACKERS:	
Any Bread	1 Slice	Graham	2
Bagel	1/2	Matzoh	1/2
Small Roll	1	Melba Toast	4
English Muffin	1/2	Oysterettes	20
Tortilla	1	Pretzels	8 Small
		RyeKrisp	3
CEREALS:		Saltines	5
Hot Cereal	1/2 Cup		
Dry Falkes	2/3 Cup	DESSERTS:	
Dry Fluffed	1 Cup	Sherbert (Fat Free)	1/2 Cup
Bran	5 Tbs.	Angelfood Cake	2 In. Sq.
Wheatgerm	2 Tbs.		
Pasta	1/2 Cup	ALCOHOL:	
Rice	1/2 Cup	Beer	5 Oz.
		Whiskey, Vodka	1 Oz.
		Gin	1 Oz.
		Wine, Dry	3 Oz.
		Wine, Sweet	2 Oz.

PROTEIN: 6 PORTIONS DAILY

Beef, Lamb, Pork	1 Oz.	Tuna (water)	1/4 Cup
Veal, Poultry	1 Oz.	Salmon (drained)	1/4 Cup
Fish	1 Oz.	Eggs	1
Lobster Tail	1 Small	Cheese, Hard	1/2 Oz.
Oysters, Clams	5 Med.	Cheese, Cottage	1/4 Cup
Shrimp	5 Med.	Peanut Butter	2 Tsp.

MILK: 2 PORTIONS DAILY

Buttermilk, Fat Free	1 Cup	Skim Milk	1 Cup
Low Fat Milk	1 Cup	Yogurt, Plain	3/4 Cup

FATS: 2 PORTIONS DAILY

Avocado	1/8 Med.	Bacon, Crisp	1 Slice
Butter	1 Tsp.	Margarine	1 Tsp.
French Dressing	1 Tbs.	Roquefort Dressing	2 Tsp.
Thousand Is. Dress.	2 Tsp.	Mayonnaise	1 Tsp.
Oil	1 Tsp.	Walnuts	6
Olives	5		

An easy way to keep track of what you should be eating daily is to keep a chart and simply check foods off as you go through the day.

> VEGETABLES ✔ ✔ ✔
> FRUITS ✔ ✔ ✔
> STARCHES ✔ ✔ ✔
> PROTEIN ✔ ✔ ✔ ✔ ✔ ✔
> MILK ✔ ✔
> FATS ✔ ✔
> EXERCISE (in 5-minute segments) ✔ ✔ ✔ ✔ ✔ ✔

How to Arrange Your Foods

Here is an example of how you can arrange your foods:

	vegetables	fruits	starches	protein	milk	fats
BREAKFAST		1	1	1		
LUNCH	1	1	1	2	1	1
DINNER	2	1	1	3	1	1
Totals	3	3	3	6	2	2

This example can be compared to a menu as follows:

BREAKFAST: 1 Fruit = 1/2 cup of orange juice
 1 Starch - 1 slice of toast
 1 Protein = 1 egg

LUNCH: 1 Vegetable = 1 cup of mixed salad
           1 Fruit = 1/3 honeydew melon

           1 Starch = 2 graham crackers
           2 Protein = 1/2 cup cottage cheese
           1 Milk = 3/4 cup plain yogurt

DINNER: Vegetables = 1/2 cup broccoli,
                       sliced tomato and cucumber
           1 Fruit = 1 peach
           1 Starch = 3 oz. dry white wine
           3 Protein = 3 oz. roast chicken
           1 Milk = 1 cup low-fat milk
           1 Fat = 1 tsp. mayonnaise

Here is a sample diet for those people who never eat breakfast:

LUNCH: Salad made with fresh vegetables and a 1/4 cup of tuna and salad dressing.
           Two slices of toast.
           1 cup of low-fat milk.

DINNER: 1/2 grapefruit
           Broiled steak (5 oz.), choice of vegetables, and salad with salad dressing.
           1/2 cup fat-free lime sherbert

SNACK: 1-1/2 cups of fresh strawberries with whipped yogurt.

As you will see, the foods have been used in a different way, but the total allocation of vegetables, fruits, starches, protein, milk, and fats remain the same. And none of the free foods were used, although we could have if the planner had wished to do so.

Remember, you can "mix and match" any way you want to. You can save all your protein for dinner or eat it for breakfast.

THE SECOND HOUR:
Practicing Self-Hypnosis

Mastering any new skill takes practice, and if you are really serious about succeeding—whether in learning an exercise routine or a new sport, programming a computer or knitting a sweater—you practice until you get it right.

That's the way it is with mastering the hypnotic response. You practice the basic techniques—you condition yourself with mental exercises until you feel comfortable with them—and *then* you use them to help you quit smoking. Contrary to what you might expect with learning other skills, the techniques involved with self-hypnosis are the easiest, most pleasant activities you could ever hope to practice. From mastering the art of relaxation to learning how to hypnotize yourself in just a few minutes, the step-by-step conditioning exercises presented in chapters 6 and 7 will not only leave you feeling rested and receptive to self-hypnosis, but will also, when you move on to chapter 8, help you produce a more positive response to the hypnotic suggestions that you stop smoking forever.

6

Understanding the Value of the Relaxation Response

Relaxation—the ability to rid the body of tension and anxiety—is an essential part of this program. Picture an empty milk bottle outside in the rain, filling up with water. When it's full, you pick up the bottle and pour the water away. In hypnosis, relaxation is like that, alleviating or draining away anxiety or tension. You'll be using relaxation before, during, and after self-hypnosis, for three distinctly different, but equally marvelous effects it has on mind and body.

Setting the Stage

The first, and most obvious benefit of relaxation occurs when it's used as a prelude to self-hypnosis—setting the stage and giving you a better chance to perform well at it.

Most people perform better at anything when they come to it relaxed. Relaxation keeps the way open for you to do your best—in sports, public speaking, dealing with conflicts, or any other situation where there is potential stress. Breaking bad habits or ingrained behavior patterns is just such a situation, and it is natural to experience some degree of tension and anxiety about the prospect of quitting smoking.

Relaxation and Hypnosis, A Winning Combination

The second benefit of being relaxed occurs when hypnosis is under way, making you more receptive to the suggestions given, and thus allowing them to sink into your subconscious mind.

A person's thinking is split between two different levels—conscious and subconscious. There is always some degree of conscious mental activity going on when a person is in a normal waking state. The more relaxed you become, the more you lower that activity so that thoughts, ideas, and, in the case of hypnosis, suggestions can easily pass into the subconscious.

Mastering the ability to relax also helps build confidence and trust that the program will succeed. As will be demonstrated in chapter 8, one of the ways self-hypnosis works is to make you more susceptible, or receptive, to suggestions—in this case, suggestions intended to convince you of your ability to stop smoking. This receptivity is not going to be instant or immediate; rather, it builds in gradual stages, increasing as *you yourself* demonstrate your ability to do what is suggested. Thus, when relaxation is the first of such suggestions—and you release yourself to the pleasant sensations that are asked of you—you become more receptive to trying the next suggestion, without critical analysis or censorship. By telling yourself you'll be more relaxed, that you'll feel heavy, or limp, or as if you were floating free, and then by actually experiencing those feelings, you are building trust. And by the time you tell yourself you'll no longer have a desire to smoke—that you'll refuse a cigarette when it's offered to you—you'll be ready and capable to *do just that*.

Relaxation and Reinforcement

The third benefit of relaxation occurs after the self-hypnosis session, when it becomes a powerful reinforcement of the program by providing the same effect you sought when smoking cigarettes—i.e., feeling calmer and more relaxed. This effect is achieved through posthypnotic suggestion; that is, telling yourself *during* hypnosis that you will return to a state of relaxation *later*, whenever you feel tension or anxiety. In other words, you put your subconscious on guard, so that if you beome nervous or tense, upset for any reason whatsoever, you will be ready to relax instantly. In this capacity, relaxation makes the need for cigarettes obsolete.

Relaxation in the reinforcement phase of the program is covered further in chapters 9 and 10. As described here, you can understand why relaxation is a fundamental strategy at all stages of quitting smoking. Start now by playing your prerecorded tape of the following exercise, which will train you to relax at will. Then, resume reading on p. 75.

HYPNOTIC EXERCISE 1

Taping Time: Approximately 20–25 minutes

Now, just make yourself comfortable. Make yourself comfortable and... close your eyes. Just allow yourself to become limp. Limp and slack. Allow all the muscles in your body to become limp and slack. Begin to take notice of your breathing. Notice the movement as you breathe in... and out. Notice the movement as you breathe in... the air filling your lungs... the upward movement of your chest.

Breathe a little deeper now. Feel the difference, and notice also that as you exhale, the air slowly leaves your lungs and your chest returns to normal rest. So breathe smoothly... somewhat deeply... steadily. Each time you breathe out and feel the breath quietly exhale from your body, you feel yourself sinking lower into a relaxed calmness. As you continue to breathe in this fashion, deliberately allowing yourself to sink down each time you exhale, you will notice this particular rhythm: That each time you exhale, you associate the air leaving your lungs with the sensation of pleasantly sinking deeper and deeper. And as you do this, you begin to become sensitive to the tension in your muscles. Breathe in, and as you exhale, release that tension.

Do it again. Breathe in... and as you exhale, release the tension.

Focus your mind on one area of your body. Start from your toes to your ankles. Breathe in, and as you allow the air to smoothly escape, release the muscles and the tensions from that area. Again, from your toes to your ankles. Breathe in... and as you release your breath, so relax all the tensions, all of the stress, all strength from the area of your toes to your ankles. Now your mind can encompass a greater area, from your toes to your thighs. Visualize the area from your toes to your thighs. And this time, as you inhale, get ready so that when you exhale you can allow every muscle, every fiber, every nerve, to relax from your toes to your thighs. Now breathe in... now exhale and let the relaxation take place.

Again. Breathe in. Now exhale, and let the relaxation take place.

Now visualize the area from your toes, all the way up into your chest, including the muscles in your back. Visualize that whole area—from your toes, all the way to your chest. Now again: Breathe... in... and exhale, and relax, from your toes to your chest. Including all of the muscles in your back.

Once again, inhale... and exhale... and relax.

And finally, visualize your whole body. From your toes. To your thighs. To your chest. Throughout your back, including your shoulders. Your neck. Your head. Your face... Even the small muscles in your jaw. Visualize your whole body. And now inhale... and slowly exhale, as you feel your whole body sinking down and down in comfort. In relaxation. In limpness.

And once more, inhale. And exhale. Sinking down and down. And now you will slowly become aware of a lazy feeling of heaviness. Become sensitive to this feeling... as if you were growing heavier, and heavier. And as you become heavier, you are sinking down and down... deeper and heavier. Heavier and deeper. The relaxation slowly, pleasantly drifting through you. The limpness pleasantly drifting all through you. The heaviness gradually drifting all through you.

Soon you will begin to listen to this tape completely at ease, enjoying the feelings described to you... enjoying the feelings of deep relaxation that are becoming so pleasant to you. For while I talk to you, you can just listen. There is nothing else for you to do. Nothing at all but just listen. Just imagine that all around you, comfortably surrounding you, is the soft cushioning of relaxation. Let this circle of peacefulness allow you just to float and drift and relax without tensions, without stress, without anxiety, without cares... just floating, relaxing. Doing absolutely nothing at all. And you will find that you *are* gradually relaxing. Just listen. It relaxes you. It makes you feel as if the pleasant heaviness is spreading all through you. Your body relaxing..: to feelings of pleasant heaviness. You feel so comfortable you're able to listen to me without any effort at all.

You are drifting further and further away from anxieties... from tensions... from stress. And you are drifting closer and closer to perfect comfort and calmness. You may become so comfortable now, so much at ease... the feelings may be so pleasant to you that you may have no desire to move. You only want to rest deeper... and deeper... Just rest deeper and deeper. You have now reached a certain degree of relaxation... but you can reach even deeper stages. Listen, and you can reach even deeper and deeper stages of wonderful, restful relaxation.

Imagine a flight of stairs. Think of them. The stairs are wide, and they are very safe. There are ten stairs, and you are standing on the top step. And now, one step at a time, you are going to slowly and safely descend the stairs. And with each step, you will descend into a deeper and deeper... and deeper... stage of profound, restful relaxation.

So now the first step. Slowly descend the first, and relax down, and down. Peaceful. Comfortable. Restful. And now the second step. Relax down. Peaceful. Your body and your mind calm... comfortable. And now the third step. Slowly floating down, and down. And now, remember your breathing. As before, as you exhale, feel yourself sinking down.

Think of the next step. As you go down the fourth step, think of it in the same way, the same time, as you exhale. So now take a nice breath ...and as you exhale, you go down the fourth step. And now another breath. And as you exhale, you go down the fifth step. And now another breath. And as you exhale, you go down the sixth step. Another breath. And as you exhale, you go down the seventh step. Another breath. And down the eighth step. And another breath. And down the ninth...

Another breath... all the way down to the tenth step. All the way down....

Now, just float. Float as if you were floating on a big, billowy cloud. Soft and comfortable. Just float. Do nothing. Just completely relax now. Deeper and deeper. And as you relax, as you feel relaxed, all of the feelings, all of the sensations of relaxation that you were told you would feel, you are feeling. And as you relax, and as you feel relaxed, all of the feelings, all of the sensations of heaviness that you were told you would feel, you are feeling. Do not resist it. Let yourself enjoy it. Relaxation is beneficial to you. You feel at peace... no stress, no strain. No anxiety. And as you relax, as you float, sometimes it may feel as if you are drifting away from everything around you. And if you feel this pleasant sensation, don't bother to analyze it.

Don't bother to analyze your thoughts, or your sensations. Just allow your mind to be passive, and allow the feeling of quietness to surround you with its protectiveness.

Now a feeling of complete relaxation is gradually stealing into your whole body. Let the muscles of your feet and ankles relax completely now. Let them go limp. And slack. Now the muscles in your legs. Let them go. You're able to do so now, easier, and easier. Let them go limp... and completely slack.

Completely relax and you can feel the feelings of heaviness in your legs, as though your legs are becoming as heavy as lead. And as you feel these feelings, your relaxation is gradually becoming deeper and deeper. Spreading all through your body. Let your stomach muscles relax. Let them go limp and slack. Now the muscles of your chest. Let them go limp and slack. And as you do so, you can feel the feelings of heaviness ... the heaviness spreading all through you. As if your whole body is becoming as heavy as lead. As if it wants to sink down, deeper and deeper. Just let your body go... heavy... heavy as lead. Just let it sink back comfortably, deeper and deeper. As it does so, you are drifting, drifting into a deeper and deeper state of profound, of total relaxation. Just give yourself up completely to this pleasant, relaxed, drowsy, comfortable feeling. As this feeling is spreading into the muscles of your neck, your shoulders, and your arms, the neck muscles relax... the muscles in the back of your neck, they relax. Let them go limp, and slack. The muscles in your shoulders ... they go limp and slack. All through your arms. The relaxation always deeper and deeper. It spreads and deepens all over your body. Relax... even more and more deeply. And you can feel the peacefulness and the benefits of deep and profound relaxation. And you will now be able to enjoy the benefits of relaxation in your everyday life. For you will find yourself calmer, more relaxed. More composed.

In a few moments, you will count to seven. And then you will open your eyes. You will feel wide awake. You will feel completely relaxed. And mentally and physically calm and composed. So gradually, you can begin to return to a state of normal activity. And as you do, the feelings of heaviness, of limpness, of lethargy will completely and totally disappear.

Now count, and with each number you will become more and more awake... calm, composed, and wonderfully relaxed.

One... two... three... four... five... six ... seven. Wide awake now. Wide awake.

Now pick up with your reading.

How did you do?

If you felt at all tense or resistant to the preceding exercise, that's perfectly normal. Between the prospect of quitting smoking and practicing something that's entirely new (as hypnosis and relaxation are to most people), many people find that the harder they try to relax, the less they are able to make it happen. Instead of trying so hard, take a passive or relaxed attitude. Just tell yourself you're going to see how you do, and don't worry about achieving anything. Pushing yourself isn't going to help.

When you are relaxing and listening to the script, don't worry if your mind wanders. Actually, this is a good sign that you are relaxed. Don't let it get you all agitated, thinking that maybe you've missed something important and now the program isn't going to work for you. It will. Letting your mind wander during hypnosis is no different from thinking about something else while you're in your car. You're probably still driving as safely and effectively as ever. So if you catch yourself wandering off, don't worry that it's going to interfere with what you're doing. Just calmly bring your focus of attention back again.

7

Hypnosis and Self-Hypnosis— A Powerful Force for Good

The "As If" Principle

Webster's Dictionary defines *to hypnotize* as "to entrance or overcome by suggestion"—a process that can be explained with the following analogy.

If you were to observe an audience watching a very suspenseful film—something like *Jaws* or *Fatal Attraction* or *The Shining*—at first you would notice everyone settled into their seats, relaxed and ready to be entertained. As the movie progressed and the suspense began to build, you would begin to notice several different reactions. Some of those watching the film would begin to tense up, and when something terrible finally happened, become visibly startled, perhaps even shouting out suddenly, hiding their eyes, or even getting up out of their seats. They would be reacting *as if* what they saw on the screen were really happening, while others in the audience would remain as relaxed as ever, munching their popcorn and calmly shaking their heads at the incredible nature of what they were seeing on the screen. Whatever the action, the doubters would maintain their sense of disbelief.

Of course what happens in the movie doesn't *really* happen—and *of course* those who react know it is only a movie, but for a few hours, they allow themselves to step out of their own reality and into the story the moviemakers would have them believe. They do it by using their imagination, and indeed, when the movie ended and the lights came up, you would see from the smiles on their faces that the believers in the audience got a great deal more entertainment out of the film than the disgruntled doubters!

The success of all popular films, novels, plays, and readings on the radio is measured by the ability to draw the audience in; that is, to elicit a response *as if* the action were really happening. Analyzing and tearing everything apart destroys the response, while suspending disbelief and criticism allows one to believe in everything that is going on.

Hypnosis succeeds on exactly this same *as if* principle. The person becomes so absorbed in what is suggested that he or she produces a response that is just *as if* these suggestions really were true. When heavy cigarette smokers are told in hypnosis that they will absolutely refuse a cigarette when one is offered, and be very proud of themselves for doing this, the more absorbed in the suggestion they are able to become—clearing the mind and suspending disbelief without censoring the suggestion—the better their chance of breaking their smoking habit. By the same token, if the person trying to quit smoking reacts to the hypnotic suggestion by saying, "But that's impossible; there's no way I'll not want that cigarette and take it," they are reacting just as those people in the movie theater who kept saying, "It's only a movie, it's not a real shark, these things aren't really happening." By looking at their own abilities critically or analytically, they reduce the chance of producing a positive hypnotic response. If they really wanted to create one, they would willingly let go of their critical judgment.

Putting the "As If" Principle to Work for You in Self-Hypnosis

By purchasing this book and reading this far, you are obviously receptive to the idea of using hypnosis to quit smoking. How will it happen? Very simply, you become hypnotized when your attention span is narrowed so you become less interested in surrounding thoughts or events. Your interest is narrowed, and the hypnotist—in this case, you—are able to paint pictures with words, stirring the imagination by conjuring up associations that connect with prior experiences.

For example, if a hypnotist were to ask a person to envision his arm becoming numb because of some impending surgery, he wouldn't just use the word numb. He would relate the sensation to a prior experience of the individual. He might ask questions such as, Have you had a tooth filled? Have you had novocaine? Did you remember the feeling you had in your jaw? Then he would attempt to transfer that feeling to the arm. There is always an association.

Now, obviously, no one is going to tell you to use this book to get through surgery without anesthesia! There are approximately fifty different levels of hypnosis, or susceptibility, and it would take far more training than a book could offer to progress to the level where you could rely on hypnosis to reduce pain. With the program in this book, you can easily reach your goal of becoming a nonsmoker on what would approximately be the seventeenth level of hypnosis—with total awareness of everything going on at all times.

There is another example of how relating to prior associations can be effective in hypnosis—one closer to the hypnotic exercise you will practice in a few moments.

Suppose someone asked you, "Do you enjoy eating chumblies?" It doesn't mean anything.

"What's a chumbly?" you reply.

"Well," your friend explains, "it looks like an orange and it tastes like something between an orange and a tangerine..."

Your mind is able to work with these associations and you begin to formulate a picture of what a "chumbly" might be.

Now, suppose that a hypnotist were to say to you, "I want you to concentrate on what I am saying. I want you to hold your arms out straight in front of you." (That's an instruction.) "Now I'm going to cause your right arm to feel heavy. (That's putting an idea into the mind of the subject.) "Can you imagine, hanging from the wrist of your right arm, a metal bucket with its handle over your wrist. (That's painting a picture of the bucket.) And gradually, sand is pouring into the bucket, making it heavier. (That's a suggestion.) Your arm is becoming tired; as tired as if you were carrying a heavy suitcase. (That's making the association with a prior experience.)

If the subject is willing to free his imagination and go with what is suggested, gradually the arm will begin to lower, and the hypnotist will have initiated the first area of susceptibility. Not gullibility, but susceptibility. The hypnotist has stirred the individual's imagination, and the individual accepts, without critical judgment, the fact that something in what the hypnotist is saying is causing the effect. It is a very simple effect, of course, but by responding on an unconscious level to the suggestions made in hypnosis, even in light hypnosis, changes can happen—habits can be broken.

There is a trap to avoid with the "as if" principle. It has to do with letting go of what *could* happen, and believing that it *will* happen. Many people who try to quit smoking become preoccupied with situations where they might fail and have a cigarette. "What's going to happen if I get upset?" "What's going to happen if I see my friend who smokes?" "What's going to happen when I have a beer at the party Saturday night?" That sort of thing. If they failed previously at their goal of being an ex-smoker in any of these situations, they are naturally going to believe it will happen again. They become overly anxious because they only have their experiences of failure to relate to, which is a terrific way of setting themselves up for failure.

This time, however, is going to be different. This time, there is hypnosis. In hypnosis you focus only on the present. You allow yourself to believe you can do anything, you become absorbed in the suggestions that you can quit, and you respond to those suggestions by resisting the urge to smoke. And by letting the urge pass with each small increment of time (a minute, an hour, a day) slowly you begin to create a new past experience based not on your failures, but rather on your success as a nonsmoker. This will be covered in more detail during the third hour of the program, when hypnosis has been completed.

How Does It Feel To Be Hypnotized?

This is one of the first questions people who use our Petrie Method programs always ask.

That pleasant, tranquil feeling you experienced during the relaxation exercise in the previous chapter, combined with the focused concentration you will practice in the exercise below, are what you can relate to in hypnosis. If you think of degrees of sleep—from a state of dozing off to a deep sleep—you will have some idea of the sensations that accompany hypnosis. On a scale of one to ten, with number one being completely and totally awake and number ten being completely and totally unconscious, the normal sleep state would occur around level seven or eight. Hypnosis occurs around level four or five. It is very similar to what you often feel just before you fall asleep—peaceful and relaxed. In hypnosis, your mind might wander as if you were daydreaming or dozing, but that is normal; it will not impair your response to the suggestions that are being made. You will hear ordinary sounds, of course—a truck rumbling down the street, or a car blowing its horn, or people talking as they pass by the window, for example. But sound does not disturb the hypnotic state or your ability to respond, as long as you hear the suggestions being made.

As for your *ability* to be hypnotized in this program (another concern of people who are new to hypnosis), you need not worry about that at all. Some people come to our seminars having taken various tests for hypnotic susceptibility—rolling the eyes up into the head, for example—and, getting a poor response, assume they are poor candidates for hypnosis. That kind of test is not useful or necessary in this book. All you need is the honest, firm intention that you want to become a permanent nonsmoker.

We know from the popularity of our seminars, and from follow-up progress reports, that the program presented in this book works for the vast majority, and that the degree of hypnotic response is but one variable in that success rate. Participants who question the success of their hypnotic response, even when it is a very good hypnotic response—insisting they didn't "feel" anything, or that their response should have been better—usually are insincere in ther motivation to stop smoking and are looking for reasons to fail. What they are really saying is, "I can't respond well enough to hypnosis; I won't be able to quit."

If you find yourself falling into this trap when you practice the exercises, you should stop and reevaluate the strength or sincerity of your commitment to quit.

The Hidden Power of the Program

In your favor, there is another, very powerful aspect of using hypnosis to become a nonsmoker. Your subconscious mind is going to respond to the suggestions that you stop smoking even if your conscious mind questions it. That's because, with hypnosis, the individual does not have to consciously think about causing something to happen in order for it to happen. When someone under hypnosis is told, for example, that his blood pressure will go down, it will happen even though the person does not know how to do it, because his subconscious mind is what relates to the suggestion.

So you have everything to gain by trying hypnosis, and nothing to lose. There is no danger of making things worse; no one ends up smoking more because of this program, and no one remains in a hypnotic state forever—enjoyable as that might be!

Preparation for Hypnotic Exercise 2

With this next exercise, which you have already recorded, imagine you were practicing to be a "method" actor—that is, using the theatrical technique of letting go of who you are and becoming the character you are playing. This acting is based on the "As If" Principle, and you're going to play this exercise as if it were *really so*. Suspend your disbelief for the moment, worry about nothing, and just see how it feels to do what is suggested.

When you are asked to picture a bucket placed over your wrist with sand pouring into it, and your arm becoming heavier and heavier, you are going to feel that arm drop down. You are going to feel it and do it. And it's fine if you ask yourself, *How much of this am I doing deliberately, and how much of this is hypnosis?* Eventually, as you practice more and progress further into the program, you will find that your hand and arm move in any direction without your being aware of any conscious effort whatsoever—and that will answer your question. But in the early stages, if you feel you have to help the response along a little bit, just to get it started, that's much better than sitting in your seat saying to yourself, "Nothing is happening. I do not feel anything and it's not going to work."

Instead, go in the same direction that is being described. *Think* of how that bucket is going to feel—how heavy that arm is going to feel. *Think* about how it will pull the arm down. Compare the concept of heaviness with the concept of lightness, and contrast how they'd feel. If a feather were placed on your outstretched wrist, you'd know how that would feel, wouldn't you? Concentrate now on that heaviness. Use your imagination. Suspend that disbelief so you can put an impression of heaviness into your subconscious. You will find it very easy to produce the response. Now turn on your prerecorded tape and listen to Hypnotic Exercise 2. When it is over, resume reading on page 88.

HYPNOTIC EXERCISE 2

Taping Time: 15–20 Minutes

Place both of your legs flat on the floor, and extend your arms out in front of you at shoulder level. Satisfy yourself that your shoulders are even and your hands on the same plane. Remember this position; you will return to it in a few moments. Now relax your hands down to your side... make yourself comfortable... and close your eyes.

Allow yourself to become limp. Limp and slack.

Allow all the muscles in your body to become limp and slack. Begin to take notice of your breathing. Notice the movement as you breathe in... and out. Notice the movement as you breathe in... the air filling your lungs. The upward movement of your chest.

Breathe a little deeper now. Feel the difference, and notice also that as you exhale, the air slowly leaves and your chest returns to normal rest. So breathe smoothly... somewhat deeply ... steadily. And each time you breathe out and feel the breath quietly exhale from your body, you feel yourself sinking lower, into a relaxed calmness. And as you continue to breathe in this fashion, deliberately allowing yourself to sink down each time you exhale, associate the air leaving your lungs with the sensation of pleasantly sinking deeper and deeper. And as you do this, begin to become sensitive to the tensions in your muscles. Breathe in, and as you exhale, release that tension.

Do it again. Breathe in... and as you exhale, release the tension.

Focus your mind on one area of your body. Start from your toes to your ankles. Breathe in, and as you allow the air to smoothly escape, release the muscles and the tensions from that area. Again, from your toes to your ankles. Breathe in... and as you release your breath, relax all of the tensions, all of the stress, all strength from the area of your toes to your ankles. Now your mind can encompass a greater area—from your toes to your thighs. Visualize the area from your toes to your thighs. And this time, as you inhale, get ready so that when you exhale you can allow every muscle, every fiber, every nerve to relax from your toes to your thighs. Now breathe in... now exhale and let the relaxation take place.

Again. Breathe in. Now exhale, and let the relaxation take place.

Now visualize the areas from your toes, all the way up into your chest, including the muscles in your back. Visualize that whole area, from your toes all the way to your chest. Now again: Breathe in ... and exhale... relax... from your toes to your chest... including all the muscles in your back.

Once again, inhale... and exhale... and relax.

And finally, visualize your whole body. From your toes. To your thighs. To your chest. Throughout your back, including your shoulders. Your neck. Your face. Even the small muscles in your jaw. Visualize your whole body. And now inhale ... and slowly exhale as you feel your whole body sinking down and down in comfort. In relaxation. In limpness.

And once more inhale. And exhale. Sinking down and down. And now you will slowly become aware of a lazy feeling of heaviness. Become sensitive to this feeling... as if you were growing heavier, and heavier. And as you become heavier, you are sinking down and down ... deeper and heavier... the relaxation slowly, pleasantly drifting through you. The limpness pleasantly drifting all through you. The heaviness gradually drifting all through you.

You are drifting further and further away from anxieties... from tensions... from stress. And you are drifting closer and closer to perfect comfort and calmness. And if you should find yourself tensing up in any way, mentally or physically, just become aware of it... and realize that now you have the ability to completely let yourself go... to give yourself up to pleasant... relaxed... drowsy... comfortable feelings. You may find your mind wandering away to other thoughts. Remember... that is all right... it won't in any way impair your response. And when you find your mind wandering, just bring it back to the sound of this tape...

Feel your body relaxing... and with the count from five to one, feel yourself descend with each of the numbers into a deeper state of relaxation. So... letting yourself go now. Five... feel yourself drifting down. Four... further... and further... down. Three... letting yourself go... down. Two... down... one... nice and calm... nice and relaxed.

Slowly extend your arms as you did before ... holding them out straight and even in front of you at shoulder level. Satisfy yourself that your arms are even, and close your eyes again...

And now imagine that a large, empty bucket has been placed over the wrist of your right arm. Its handle rests on your wrist and the bucket dangles down beneath your arm. And as you hold your arms outstretched, sand begins to pour into the bucket. Slowly... slowly... slowly at first, and then more rapidly. Now it is filling the bucket... up to the halfway point. And your arm is resisting the weight of the bucket... as more sand pours in. And the bucket is three-quarters full... Your muscles are feeling the weight increasing, and your wrist is getting very, very tired. Now the bucket is filled with sand

...and you give in to the tremendous heaviness it has created in your right arm... You feel your arm being drawn down...and down...and down...toward your side.

Now open your eyes...and look at your arms, and continue reading.

Has your right arm moved down—even a few inches? Did you feel it moving down? Concentrating all your attention on the image of that heavy pail, you may not have even felt the arm lowering.

And if you found your arm higher, which can happen in some instances, it's a sign that there's some resistance. You need to let go. Practice it again, and this time, don't try to resist it.

To encourage a positive response, think of a bucket that's twice the size of the one you were imagining, with twice as much sand pouring into it. In seminars, when a person who's succeeded with this exercise draws on a blackboard what he's pictured, his bucket is double the size of those who had a lesser response.

Now we move on to the next prerecorded exercise—an exercise that further develops your receptivity to suggestions.

The Finger-Lifting Exercise

Can you hypnotize yourself in just a few minutes? Of course you can. Here's an exercise that will prove it. Rest your hands on your thighs, palms down, close your eyes, and concentrate all your attention on one finger. You are going to lift that finger off your leg with no conscious effort or awareness. Yes, it will really happen. Now listen to Hypnotic Exercise 3. Then resume reading on page 90.

HYPNOTIC EXERCISE 3
Taping Time: Approximately 3–5 Minutes

Sit straight and comfortably, feet together on the floor. Breathe slowly and deeply. Close your eyes.

Rest your hands on your thighs, palms down. Be very aware of your hands. Feel their weight on your thighs... and feel their warmth. Concentrate on their weight. Concentrate all your senses on a possible weight difference. Does one hand feel lighter than the other? One hand will feel lighter than the other if you are keenly aware of the slightest difference in sensation.

As soon as one hand feels lighter, concentrate on the lightness of this hand. Concentrate on every slight difference in sensation. Feel the sensations. Feel the transfer of heat from your hand to your leg. Feel the texture of the clothing on which the hand is resting. Concentrate, always concentrate, on the sensation of lightness. On the feeling of warmth. On the feeling of texture. Concentrate on the tingling sensation, if you feel it. Concentrate on any and all sensations you feel in this light, very light hand.

Now concentrate even more. Center all your concentration on one finger—your index finger. Your index finger is now extremely light. You feel all those sensations... texture... warmth ... tingling... that you felt in the hand. Concentrate now on one more image, and then something is going to happen.

Think of your heavy hand as one side of an old-fashioned scale—the kind of scale where one side goes down, and the other side rises. Your heavy hand is causing the lighter hand to rise. You feel the force to rise in your index finger. You know that this finger will rise. You feel it pressing less and less on your leg. Slowly, as the scales tip, you feel it lifting.

Now open your eyes, and resume reading the book.

Look at your right hand. What do you see?

Most people find a very definite rise of the index finger on their first try. Some get just a slight, or almost imperceptible rise. Everybody gets more of a response the second time. In repeating the exercise, greater contact is made with the subconscious mind.

Still greater contact can be made if, after you have received a good signal from one finger, you expand the lightness sensation to the other fingers of the lighter hand. You can get other fingers to rise, too. In fact, you can concentrate on the palm of your hand, on your wrist, and on your entire arm, and the whole arm will levitate.

Whatever part of the arm you levitate, be it one finger, many fingers, the whole hand or limb, it is your subconscious mind activating the nerves that causes it to happen. And by doing this exercise, you have proven that your subconscious mind is in close touch with your conscious mind—can actually will things to happen without your even being aware of it.

HYPNOTIC EXERCISE 4 (Do not prerecord)

The Amazing Pendulum Response

Your next exercise is a variation of the Chevreul Pendulum Exercise that has existed for over 150 years. It is not a taped exercise at all, but something you will concentrate on with your eyes open.

For our purposes, the Chevreul Pendulum Exercise demonstrates how strong your response to a suggestion can be when you let go of your critical judgment and analysis.

To do this exercise, those who attend our Quit-Smoking Seminars use a small weight about the size of a pea, suspended from a chain. You can substitute a pendant hanging from a necklace, or a small screw tied to a six- to eight-inch length of thread. Carefully trace the circle below onto a plain white piece of paper so it will lie flat.

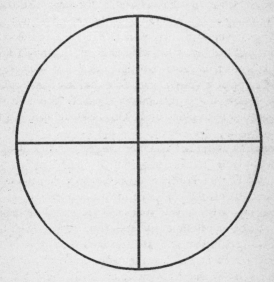

Using only your thoughts, using only your concentration, you are going to *will* that screw to begin to swing around in a perfect circular motion, following the circumference of the circle. You will see that it will actually happen.

Just place the paper on a flat surface—a desk or a

countertop—in front of you, with the circle facing up. Hold the thread between your thumb and forefinger so that the screw is suspended about an inch over the circle. Relax, and find a comfortable position, resting your elbows on the table if you wish.

Concentrate all of your attention on the screw at the end of the chain, and as you stare at it, using only your thoughts, only your concentration, *will* that piece of hardware to swing around in a circle. Give it time... relax... give it time. And you will find it is beginning to swing around in a perfect circle!

Now visualize the screw changing directions, and beginning to swing back and forth along the perfect straight line. And once again, using only your thoughts and your concentration, *will* that screw to swing in a perfect straight line.

Pick another direction. No figure eights or squares, but rather a circle, a straight line, or a diagonal, and *will* the screw to go in the direction you want. Use just your thoughts and concentrate on it. Go ahead and give it a try.

If you are surprised it really works, you shouldn't be. What you have done is demonstrate to yourself your ability to put the "As If" Principle to work for you, just the way it was described at the beginning of this chapter.

You may have felt as if your hand and arm were moving with no conscious effort. But they *were* moving with conscious effort! In the exercise, you thought only about the weight—not about your hand and arm. You put your critical judgment aside and let your mind really believe it was controlling the weight. You stopped worrying about whether you were doing it on purpose—and as soon as you stopped thinking about it, your hand *did* move the screw in a circle. It *did* move the screw back and forth on a diagonal, and in a straight line. Your mental powers had nothing to do with it!

That's the whole point. You *are* suggestible. You are able

to suspend your critical analysis to a significant degree, and the ability to perform this hand and arm movement indicates that you have reached the level of hypnosis necessary to produce behavioral change. It is the level of response you need to be able to quit smoking easily, free of worry about whether or not the exercises and the suggestions are working. The pendulum response demonstrates that you are able to just let the results happen.

And now you are ready to begin the hypnosis that, through suggestions, will provide the means to quit smoking. Before you proceed, tell yourself that you won't analyze the suggestions. When you hear the suggestions on the tape, you will stop smoking without anxiety or cravings; you will simply accept these suggestions. Instead of saying to yourself, "It will be a miracle if this works," tell yourself that you *know* it will work. You expect nothing less. This is an investment that you are making for yourself.

THE THIRD HOUR:
Putting Hypnosis to Work for You—Now It's Time to Quit

Now you are ready to realize your greatest wish—to become a nonsmoker once and for all.

In the first hour of this program, you read chapters 1–5 to prepare for hypnosis, securing in your mind a new motivation to quit.

In the second hour, you read chapter 6 and 7 to master the simple techniques of relaxation and become familiar with variations of the basic hypnotic response. Everything that you were told would happen *did* happen; you experienced all of the interesting and pleasant effects of the hypnotic responses you practiced. You learned quickly how easy it is to reach the level of hypnosis you need to quit smoking.

The third hour of the program is about to begin. By participating in the hypnotic exercises given in chapter 8—exercises that naturally and easily progress from what you have already learned—you will make your goal happen. You will put powerful suggestions into your subconscious mind that will free you forever from your habit of smoking cigarettes. In other words: *When you have finished reading chapter 8, you will have quit smoking.* And when you finished reading chapters 9 and 10, you will have all the reinforcement techniques you need to succeed at quitting, *forever.*

8

Your Hour to Stop Smoking

The exercises you practiced in chapters 6 and 7—relaxing at will, lowering your arm, lifting your finger, and swinging the pendulum—were the first building blocks in creating a strong hypnotic response. Now you are going to increase that response. In other words, you are going to strengthen your ability to receive hypnotic suggestions on a deeper level of your subconscious. To achieve this, you are going to do exactly what the participants of our seminars do—experience one segment of hypnosis, take a break, and then experience a second, slightly longer segment of hypnosis. Known as "fractional hypnosis," this process of becoming hypnotized in several small increments of time, rather than in one longer, continuous session, provides the opportunity to increase the level of concentration, to build up a little **bit** more of response with each segment. Ultimately, it gives participants the chance to achieve their strongest possible response to hypnotic suggestions. The success rate with this approach in our Quit-Smoking Seminars proves that it really works.

By using hypnosis this way now, you will permanently fix into your subconscious all the suggestions you need to stop smoking.

A Note about the Hypnotic Suggestions You Will Be Using

Each of us has a unique view of the world; one person sees the glass as being half full, the other sees it as half empty. In hypnosis, each person responds differently to the suggestions that are given. For some, negative suggestions have the most impact—the thought that inhaling a cigarette is like inhaling poison or mucus, for example. The picture in their mind is disgusting to be sure, but it is an effectively repulsive suggestion. For others, positive suggestions work best—for example, the idea that as a nonsmoker, you'll feel stronger, healthier, more invigorated in all your activities.

Most people respond to both positive and negative suggestions, but they are more receptive to one category than the other. You know who you are, simply by how you reacted to the examples described. In this program, you won't need to worry about tailoring the hypnotic suggestions to fit your individual personality—your subconscious will do it for you. It will absorb both the positive and negative suggestions, but those having the greatest impact will stay in your mind long after the hypnosis has been completed.

You are about to listen to Hypnotic Exercise 5. When it is over resume reading on page 107.

A Note on the Audio tapings for Chapter 9. You will need a blank, sixty-minute tape to record the scripts from this chapter which you will have done *before* you begin the three-hour session. Tape the first exercise (p. 99) on Side One; tape the second exercise (p. 107) on Side Two of your cassette. This will provide the time gap you will need to take a five-minute break before you flip the tape over and listen to Side Two.

HYPNOTIC EXERCISE 5
(To be taped on side one of a sixty-minute audio tape)

Taping Time: 20–25 Minutes

Make yourself comfortable and prepare yourself to relax. In a moment, you will take three deep breaths. And as you exhale on the third breath, you will close your eyes.

So now take your first deep breath and prepare your mind, and your body, to relax. Now take your second breath. Take a deep breath and relax a little more. And now take your third breath, and as you exhale, close your eyes. Now, comfortably, close your eyes. Keep your eyes closed.

As you sit there relaxing, listening to this tape and following its instructions, you will soon find that you are relaxing more deeply. More and more. You will find that you are relaxing deeper and deeper. Drifting down further and further into a very deeply relaxed state. Now when you hear the word *limp*, you will immediately allow all of the muscles in your body to become limp. To become soft and slack. Okay, now: Limp. Let them go limp now. Become aware of the slackness in your muscles as you let the muscles become limp. Become aware of the feeling of relaxation—restful, soothing, and quiet.

Now relax each section of your body. Begin with your feet and your ankles. Let the muscles of your feet and your ankles relax. Just let them go limp. Now let the muscles of your legs go limp and slack. And as they relax more and more, you will begin to feel a growing sensation of heaviness in your feet, and in your legs. And the limper you allow your feet and your legs to become, the more relaxed they will become. The heavier they will feel. And soon the feeling of relaxed, limp heaviness will drift into your calves, into your thighs. You will feel the sensations of relaxation. And you will feel the tensions just draining away as you relax more and more. And you will also begin to notice a feeling of comfort and security as the limp heaviness spreads through your whole body and relaxes it, deeper and deeper. You will feel all the tension just draining away. This wonderful feeling of tranquility and relaxation will spread and extend into the muscles of your abdomen, and into your chest. And you will begin to feel your whole body becoming loose and limp, and all the tensions just drifting away. Just draining away. And the feelings of relaxation flowing through your body. Flowing from your feet, into your thighs, and into your abdomen. Flowing and drifting into your chest, into your shoulders. You will feel looser and limper as you drift down into a comfortable, pleasant, relaxed tranquility. The relaxation and limpness that flows over your shoulders continues to drift down your back. And the remaining tensions drain away.

You can let yourself go completely. You can totally permit yourself to drift down deeper, and deeper. The slackness and looseness can continue to totally relax you. Feel the flow of this wonderful feeling continuing—continuing into the muscles of your neck. All of the muscles in the front of your neck, and the side of your neck become looser and limper. Just let go.

And finally, you can relax the muscles in your

face. And in your cheeks. Let the muscles relax, totally and completely. And as you continue with these feelings of relaxation, you will notice that you are beginning to feel the warmth and the heaviness that you were told you would feel. And you can now give yourself over completely to these pleasant, comfortable sensations. Your breathing has become deep and regular. Your whole body has become totally and completely quiet. Still. And comfortable.

Just listen to the tape. You do not have to concetrate intensely. All you need to do is to listen and experience the feelings suggested. And then all the suggestions that are given to you will have the effect that you want them to have. The feelings of relaxation that you are now experiencing are so pleasant to you. They are so pleasant that you do not wish to disturb them. They make you comfortable. So comfortable, in fact, that you have no desire to move. You feel perfectly content, just as you are. You can enjoy the feelings of being relaxed. Nothing else will bother you. And although you are relaxing deeper and deeper now, you will notice that you can still be aware of everything that is around you. You will also find that you can disregard anything that you wish to disregard, yet pay attention to anything that you wish to pay attention to.

Be aware that you are truly experiencing the feelings that you were told you would experience. Remember, at the beginning, you took three deep breaths and closed your eyes and relaxed your body? You were told you would relax, and you became relaxed. You are relaxed, but now you can become even more relaxed—much more deeply relaxed than you are now. The doorway to a much deeper relaxation is right in front of you now. Soon you will be guided through this doorway into a much deeper state of relaxation, and when you reach that depth, you will hear the suggestion that will cause you to achieve the very things that you wish to achieve.

Now visualize the doorway. Now begin to open the door, and as you open it, I want you to see what is beyond it. For behind the door there is a long, comfortable staircase, winding down and down. And in the dim light, you are going to begin to go down the staircase, comfortably and safely, eager to experience the feelings of deep relaxation that you will feel as you go down each step. Now begin to descend down. Slowly, one step after the other. Step. By Step. Going down deeper and deeper. Step by step, more and more comfortable. Deeper and deeper. Slowly, one step after the other. Step by step. Going down deeper and deeper. Much more comfortable. Deeper. And deeper. Until finally you have reached the bottom of the staircase.

And at the bottom there is a platform. A platform that seems to be soft and comfortable. A platform like a deep couch covered with soft cushions. And you're able to lie back on this couch, sinking down into its softness. And as you do, it begins to drift slowly, as if it were floating. Just floating and drifting. And you become aware of the whole feeling of the movement—the warmth, the comfort, and the drowsiness, as you keep drifting and drifting.

As you drift, you remember that when you were walking down the staircase, you were really going into a deeper and deeper state, so you would be able to respond to the suggestions I am going to give you. And that each step really represented a deeper state of response. So when you reached the bottom, you were in as deep a state as you needed to be; as deep a state as necessary to respond to the suggestions—the suggestions that will be given to you. These suggestions will take hold quickly and easily, and your mind will make use of the suggestions automatically, whenever you need them. These suggestions will make the changes that will bring you total and absolute success.

For now, as you continue to listen to this tape, all of the suggestions you receive will make the changes that we want them to make. And because of the suggestions, you will have no more need or desire to smoke. You will have no cravings for cigarettes. You will no longer have the impulsive habit of smoking. The pattern of habit that you had to smoke is being erased now. You will not need to reach for a cigarette because you are tense or bored or nervous.

No matter what the reason was that you started to smoke, no matter what the reason was that you continue to smoke, it is now in the past. All of the old habits, all of the old impulses, all of the old cravings to smoke ... are in the past. The original reason you started to smoke and the reasons you continued smoking no longer matter now, and will not consciously or subconsciously influence you any longer. There is no longer any need or reason to smoke. There is no longer any impulse or craving or compulsion to smoke.

Anytime in the future you ever think of smoking, the very thought will be a signal for you to take a deep breath and to relax. And as you are relaxing, all the reasons for you not to smoke will immediately return to your mind. If at any time, the thought of smoking ever comes to you again, it will be a signal to take a deep breath, and as you exhale that breath, all the reasons not to smoke will immediately come back into your mind.

Because of the suggestions you have received, you are no longer a compulsive smoker. Because of the suggestions I have given you, there is no longer any reason for smoking. And never again will you ever try to smoke. Because you made an absolute commitment to stop smoking. You made a value judgment to stop smoking. You made a choice between a healthy life... and cigarettes, realizing that you cannot have both. You have chosen to quit smoking, and you no longer feel threatened by the thought of stopping smoking. You are determined and committed to succeed, and proud of the absolute commitment that you have made to yourself. Because you have stopped smoking, there is no further reason to think of yourself as a smoker. No further reason for trying to smoke.

By not smoking, you're going to begin living your life in a new and exciting way. Not smoking will make you happier and happier with each passing day. Visualize yourself going through the day feeling good—healthy and relaxed. Without the odor of cigarettes. Without the expense of cigarettes. Without the coughing. Without having to constantly light cigarettes. Being totally and completely free of the addiction.

You will not feel as if anything is missing from your life because you have stopped smoking. You will have more energy; you will have more concentration. You will have a greater attention span. You will be less nervous, less anxious.

Because of the suggestions you are receiving here, you will not replace the smoking habit with any other habit whatsoever. You will not replace it with overeating. You will not replace it with snacking. Your appetite will not increase. Your hunger will not increase. You will have no increase in hunger or appetite, because as a nonsmoker, you will feel healthy, complete, with nothing missing from your life.

Without the poisons of cigarettes in your body, you will become calmer, much more relaxed. You will feel calm and much more relaxed. Anytime at all in the future that you ever find yourself becoming upset or anxious or worried, or the thought of smoking comes to your mind, you need only to take a deep breath and release the breath slowly. And you will immediately relax, completely and totally. Mentally and physically. A single deep breath will automatically relax you, for your commitment not to smoke is permanent. But you will deal with it on a minute-to-minute basis. You will not be tempted by others who are smoking. You will not be tempted by situations in which you used to smoke. For you now realize that when you used to smoke, you derived nothing from smoking. Cigarettes did not calm you down. Cigarettes did not offer any escape. Cigarettes only robbed you of your energy. Dulled your senses. Constricted your blood vessels. Weakened your lungs.

You will no longer be tempted to smoke in any situation in which you were previously conditioned to smoke. Such as smoking while you were working. Or while you were driving your car. Or smoking with your coffee, or after dinner, or with a drink. Because you will never again have the craving—the desire or need to smoke.

For you now recognize that smoking was a poison to your body. The taste of smoking was poisonous. And there was no pleasure, no enjoyment from tasting poisonous gases entering your mouth, going down into your lungs and poisoning your body.

You will no longer have any pleasurable feelings from the idea of smoking. You will no longer have any pleasurable memories from smoking. Instead, you will feel healthy and proud and happy for not smoking. And in the future, if the thought of smoking ever comes to you again, you will take a deep breath and automatically relax. The thought will dissipate and disappear. And you will feel healthy and happy and proud of yourself as a nonsmoker. You *are* a nonsmoker, and never want to smoke again. You will remember cigarettes in the bad sense. The bad taste in your mouth; the odor of your breath. The smell of cigarette smoke on your clothes. The way cigarettes robbed you of energy and vitality and health. The old forces that caused you to smoke no longer control you. You are free from the temptations of smoking. Your health is recovering; your energy is returning. You have taken a positive and important step, and you feel good about yourself.

Now, in a moment, we're going to return upwards, on the same staircase, and as we return upwards, you're going to feel yourself becoming wider and wider awake. You'll become more and more alert, both mentally and physically. So now we come to the last five steps. When we get to the top step, you will open your eyes and feel wonderfully relaxed.

Now. One—drifting higher and higher, toward very normal wakefulness. Two—with a wonderful positive feeling. Three—higher and higher. Four—wider and wider awake. Five—feeling wonderfully relaxed.

Open your eyes now. Take a five-minute break.

And now we go back to the hypnosis, with the final induction. Turn your tape to Side Two. When it is over, resume reading on page 117.

HYPNOTIC EXERCISE 6

Taping time: 20–25 minutes

Just sit back comfortably. Close your eyes, and try to let yourself go as limp as you can. Try to go limp. And slack. Let all of the muscles of your body relax, and as you let the muscles relax, try to feel them relaxing. Try to be aware that they *are* relaxing. Relax them so completely that you can actually feel them relax. Don't try to hold yourself together. Let yourself go. Let the muscles of your feet, of your ankles, relax. Let the muscles of your legs...relax. Let them go limp. And slack. Once you do this, you might feel the beginning of a sense of relaxation in your feet and your legs. And the limper you allow them to go, the heavier they will become, until eventually they will feel as heavy as lead.

In the same way, let the muscles in your shoulders, in your back...let them relax. Let them relax completely. Let the muscles in your arms, and your back, let them relax. Let them go limp and slack. And as you continue these feelings of relaxation, you will begin to feel heavier. And heavier. As if you are beginning to sink down ...and down...and down.

If you feel yourself tensing in any way, either mentally or physically, just be aware of it and let yourself go. Give yourself up completely to the pleasant, relaxed, drowsy, comfortable feeling, and you will begin to experience the sensation of heaviness in your body, as if your whole body were becoming as heavy as lead.

Now that you are beginning to relax, listen quietly to the tape. You don't have to do anything. Just be aware of the sound of it. You don't have to concentrate on it. Just be aware of it, and feel your body relaxing. You will relax more and more, and all the suggestions that you are given will have the effect that we want them to have. As you continue to relax, and as you continue to feel the heaviness, you will also feel some drowsiness, and you will also feel a feeling of comfort. You will feel comfortable. In fact, you will become so very comfortable that you will have no desire to move, no desire to think of anything. You will just want to enjoy the feelings that you have. And nothing will bother you.

As you are told that you are more comfortable, you feel more comfortable. And as you drift deeper and deeper, you will have no desire to move, or to speak, or to do anything. You need only a desire to relax, and you are relaxing. Your body is becoming very, very relaxed. You need not have any desire to move at all; only a desire to relax deeply. You will find that the feeling is very similar to drifting asleep, yet you can still hear this tape. You can hear it and ignore everything else. You are becoming more relaxed now, just as you were told you would be. You are becoming drowsier, just as you were told you would be. And all the suggestions given to you now will be completely effective.

You will hear counting now, from one to five. And as you do, you will be able to sink into a much deeper state. At the count of five, you will sink deeper. You will feel more comfortable; you will feel more drowsy.

Now. The counting begins.

One. Feel yourself sinking much deeper. Much deeper into the state of relaxation. Further and further away from all outside concerns. Just enjoy where you are. What you are doing. What you are feeling.

Two. Each number carries you down deeper, deeper, and deeper. With each word, with each moment that passes, you are able to drift deeper.

Three. Deeply, soundly. So much like when you fall asleep. Always deeper and deeper. You can feel yourself sinking into this very deep state. Sinking down and down. So comfortable, so pleasant, in which you pay attention to nothing else. Nothing else need concern you now. Nothing at all.

Four. Listening to the tape, you drift deeper. All the suggestions given to you will be very effective. You are becoming more and more responsive to the suggestions, and you will continue to become increasingly more responsive. Even as the time passes, even as you listen, you are drifting deeper and becoming more and more responsive. You will become even more responsible to all the suggestions you hear. At the next count, you will feel how much more deeply relaxed you are.

Five. Deep... deeply relaxed. You are so very deeply relaxed now that you are able to respond completely to all the suggestions that shall be given to you. And everything you are told you will feel, you *will* feel. Everything you are told is going to happen will happen exactly as it is told. You will experience every sensation that is described, exactly as it is described.

From now on, you will experience an absolute *distaste* of smoking. All the old feelings you have had of your need to smoke, of your cravings to smoke, of your desires to smoke—these old feelings will rapidly and completely diminish.

You are now turning away from your smoking addiction, and you are aware of what a positive experience it is to stop smoking.

You are beginning to feel very proud of the commitment you made to yourself to stop smoking. No longer are you, or will you ever be again, a slave to that disabling habit. You will now see other people's smoking as a weakness, and your not smoking as a strength.

You no longer have any desire to inhale the poisonous tars, the poisonous nicotine, down into your lungs, turning them black and filling them with mucus. The thought of inhaling a cigarette now will be like inhaling dirt or mucus to your mind. This thought will be so revolting to you, so disgusting to you, that your desire to stay away from cigarettes permanently completely overwhelms the old desire to smoke.

The fear of emphysema, of heart disease, of cancer; of shortness of breath; of poor circulation; of loss of energy—these fears, these feelings that every smoker experiences, reinforce your need to stay away from that terribly disabling habit.

You continue now to relax, to feel the wonderful, pleasant sensation of relaxation. Just feel the comfort of this relaxation. You have no desire to change it at all. You don't feel like changing anything. You just want the pleasantness of the relaxation. You need not pursue any other thoughts; just the feeling that you are relaxing deeper. Sinking deeper and deeper, away from everything around you. And these feelings of relaxation are bringing you greater and greater feelings of comfort as you feel yourself relaxing down... and down... sinking down deeper and deeper... as you relax deeper and deeper.

Soon you will be able to listen to this tape completely at ease, enjoying the feelings that are described. Enjoying the feelings of deep relaxation that are becoming so pleasant to you. You can just listen. There is nothing for you to do. Nothing at all but just listen. Just imagine that all around you, comfortably surrounding you, are the soft cushions of relaxation. That this circle of peacefulness allows you just to float and drift and relax. Allows you to drift and relax without tensions, without stress, without anxiety, without cares—just floating, relaxing, doing absolutely nothing at all.

And now you will find that you *are* becoming even more relaxed. Just listen to this tape; it relaxes you. It makes you feel as if a pleasant heaviness is slowly spreading through you. Your body is relaxing with feelings of pleasant, wonderful heaviness. You feel so comfortable, you're able to listen without any effort—without any effort at all. And you are drifting further and further away from stress. Drifting further from anxiety or from tension. And drifting closer and closer to perfect comfort, calmness. You may become so comfortable now, so much at ease, the feelings may be so pleasant to you, that you may not even have the desire to move. You may only want to rest... to rest deeper, and deeper, and deeper.

And as you rest, once again you think of your purpose of stopping smoking. The image of yourself now with a cigarette is a very ugly one. You will never again choose a cigarette over your own health. You will now choose your health over the cigarette. You will find it far more satisfying than any cigarette could ever be, and you will not replace the smoking habit with any other negative habit, such as overeating. In fact, your appetite will in no way increase. You will have absolutely no craving, no desire for additional food.

From now on you will have the reassuring

knowledge that you have stopped doing something detestable to yourself, and have done something very positive for yourself. You will have complete and absolute control over the old habit of smoking. There will be absolutely no circumstances in which you would choose to smoke. You realize now that the cigarette offers no escape from tensions; no escape from anxieties. You realize now that all that cigarettes have ever done for you is to slowly, sometimes painfully, eat away at your life, at your health... like a disease.

Just completely relax now, deeper and deeper. And as you relax, as you feel relaxed, all of the feelings, all of the sensations of relaxation that you were told you would feel, you are feeling. And as you relax, as you feel relaxed, all of the feelings, all of the sensations of heaviness that you were told you would feel, you are feeling. Do not resist it. Let yourself enjoy it. Relaxation is beneficial to you. You feel at peace. No stress. No strain. No anxiety. And as you relax, as you float, sometimes it may feel that you are drifting away from everything around you. And if you feel this pleasant sensation, don't bother to analyze your thoughts or sensations. Just allow your mind to be passive, and allow the feeling of quietness to surround you with its protectiveness.

Once again, bring your mind back to stopping smoking.

And now you will fully understand that by having stopped smoking, you will completely reverse the cycle of illness and disease, and begin instead the process of cleaning all of the filth, all of the damage out of your lungs, out of your body. The process of restoring your health, of repairing the damage, and restoring your strength and vitality—this is very relaxing to you to know that you're going to restore your strength; to repair the damage; to restore your health and vitality.

So as you hear counting—counting from five to one—and as you let yourself descend down with the numbers, into an even deeper state of relaxation, you will find yourself drifting further and further away from *ever* needing a cigarette again.

Listen to the counting.

Five. Let yourself drift down. Drift further and further away from ever to smoke again.

Four. Drifting lower.

Three... Two... One.

All the suggestions you have received, and all the suggestions you will receive, will be totally effective. And the strength of the suggestions will never waver. Will never lessen. They become a permanent state of mind, continuing every minute of every day. And every day now, without your cigarettes, without smoking, you will become physically and mentally stronger, fitter. Without cigarettes robbing your energy and dulling your senses, you will become more alert, awake, more energetic. And every day without the cigarettes constricting your blood vessels, forcing your heart to pump harder, you will find that your nerves grow stronger and steadier. And for the next few days, you will become so deeply interested in the pride of stopping smoking, so deeply interested in your new feelings of health, that your mind will not be preoccupied with smoking. You will only regard cigarettes with disgust. So even if the thought of a cigarette momentarily occurs to you, you will go right on with whatever you are doing, and the thought will easily pass by, no longer having *any* effect upon you. Every day without a cigarette, your mind will become calmer, clearer, more composed. You will be less easily worried or agitated. You will be able to think more clearly, and concentrate more easily. From now on, you will see cigarettes in their true perspective—as a filthy, disgusting habit. You will never again associate the thought of a cigarette with pleasure. And because you have stopped smoking, every day you will have a greater feeling of personal well-being. A greater feeling of personal safety. A greater feeling of personal security. More than you have felt for a long, long time. And every day without the cigarettes, you will become and remain more and more completely relaxed, both mentally and physically. And as you remain more relaxed, less tensed, you will develop much more confidence in yourself, much more confidence in your ability to do *whatever you have to do*—without the need of a cigarette. You will have confidence in your ability to stay away from cigarettes without fear, without anxiety, without tensions, without frustrations, without uneasiness. And because of this, every day you will feel more and more independent. Independent of the smoking habit. And you will know that no matter how difficult or trying things may be, you will be able to cope with them, easily and efficiently, without any need for a cigarette at all. And because all of these things will happen exactly as I tell you they will happen, you will feel much happier, much more content, much more cheerful, much more optimistic.

Remember, there are absolutely no cirumstances under which you will ever again choose to smoke.

Now you *are* relaxed. You are able to respond completely to all the suggestions. And everything you were told you would feel, you will feel. And everything you were told is going to happen, will happen. Exactly. And every sensation that you were told you would experience, you will experience, exactly.

Now in a few moments, we will count to seven. And at the count of seven, you will open your eyes. You will feel wide awake, and you will feel wonderfully better for this long and relaxed rest. You will feel completely relaxed, mentally and physically. You will feel calm and composed.

So, gradually now, you can begin to return to a state of normal activity. And as you do, the feelings of heaviness, of limpness, of lethargy, will completely and totally disappear.

Now, the counting begins. With each number, you can become wider and wider awake—calm, composed, and wonderfully relaxed. One, two, three, four, five, six, seven. Wake up now. Wake up.

9

The New, Nonsmoking You—Adjusting to Being a Healthy Ex-Smoker

Although you feel no different from the way you did nearly three hours ago, before you opened this book, a momentous change has occurred in your psyche. The self-hypnosis in chapter 8 has fixed into your subconscious the strongest case for quitting cigarettes that you have ever encountered. Through hypnosis, all the suggestions that you stop smoking have been absorbed, have settled deep into the recesses of your mind, and now remain firmly in place as your hidden reserve of strength in living up to your commitment as a nonsmoker. *As of today you* are *a nonsmoker.*

However, the program isn't over; at least, not quite yet. To round it out, there remain a few simple guidelines and strategies to ensure both the immediate and long-term success of the hypnosis you've just experienced. These strategies begin with the initial, critical phase of quitting, discussed here in chapter 9. During this period of time—for approximately the next six weeks—maintaining your commitment as a nonsmoker will involve the use of the reinforcement tape. You should also be prepared for certain adjustments that might be required during the days ahead. While most people do not notice any physical or mental changes as a result of giving up cigarettes, it's perfectly normal if they do occur. Knowing about these changes in advance will give you a solid base of confidence so you can deal with them easily and realistically, should the need arise.

Moving on from there, chapter 10 ensures long-term objectives with quitting, concluding the program by building a positive outlook on the future—the outlook of a triumphant, successful ex-smoker.

But let us take these phases as they occur, concentrating first on the days immediately after your three-hour stop-smoking session has ended.

The Advantages of Using a Reinforcement Tape

Of all the techniques or approaches available to help people quit smoking, the ones that have proved the most successful include some form of reinforcement—a specific strategy to carry you into the future with your motivation to remain a nonsmoker strong and intact.

Moreover, if there is enough reinforcement, the chance of doing well *for a longer period of time* becomes much better. We know this to be true by following those who have participated in our program. We ask them to listen to a reinforcement tape (the one used in their three-hour session) on a daily basis for the first forty-five days after the three-hour session, and then every other day for another month. Based on questionnaire responses, the vast majority of the people who succeeded at quitting on a long-term basis played their tapes for the full time recommended, while those who went back to smoking three months, six months, a year later, *stopped playing the tape after the first couple of days or weeks*.

The Petrie Method program that has been adapted for this book uses the exact same reinforcement that we provide for those who attend the group or private sessions—that is, the hypnotic exercise you taped and used at the end of chapter 8 (beginning on page 107). As with those who attend our group or private seminars, you, too, will play it once a day for the next forty-five days, and then every other day for another month.

It makes no difference when during the day you use the tape, or how erratic the schedule may be. It can be early in the morning one day, late at night the next day, and at noon on the day after that—but there is one important consideration: Because *listening to the tape may make you drowsy*, you should never play it when you are driving a car, using any kind of machinery, or are involved in a similar task that, for safety's sake, requires your full concentration.

Choose a time when you can sit back comfortably in a chair, or lie down and close your eyes. If you should find yourself falling asleep, missing some or all of the suggestions given on the tape but waking up at the end when you are "counted out," that's fine. It means you've actually achieved the optimum level of response, or what is termed *hypnotic sleep*. If you find yourself falling asleep and not waking up at the end of the tape, then you are going through a hypnotic sleep and into a natural one—a pleasant, unexpected catnap, perhaps, but not that conducive to reaping the benefits of hypnosis. Try playing the tape sitting up, rather than lying down, if you continue to fall asleep, or play it earlier in the day when you are not tired.

If you are interrupted while playing the tape—for example, the telephone or the doorbell rings and you can't ignore it—just count silently from one to five and bring yourself back to your full wakeful state. When you go back to the tape, start it over from the beginning. It doesn't help to pick it up again in the middle, where you left off.

Beware of overconfidence. If you feel no urge to smoke after using the reinforcement tape for a few days, it may be tempting to put it aside thinking that you no longer need it. Don't do it. No matter how confident and terrific you feel, remind yourself that you are not using the tape for what's going on in the present—you're using it to forge your way into the future, to build the foundation for remaining a nonsmoker, far beyond how you feel today. You *need* that tape—daily for the full forty-five days specified, and then every other day for the month after that.

Increasing the Effectiveness of Your Reinforcement Tape

The power of your reinforcement tape lies in its posthypnotic suggestions—that is, the suggestions presented during hypnosis that will affect what will happen later.

Posthypnotic suggestions are different from direct suggestions because of the time frame. "All of your muscles are beginning to feel heavier" is a direct suggestion because, presumably, its effect occurs during the hypnotic state. "You will be successful in quitting smoking permanently. You will not feel deprived; you will not feel anxious; you will not eat more. Your appetite and your hunger will not increase." These are posthypnotic suggestions. Their effect is intended to take place *after* hypnosis.

You can change the posthypnotic suggestions that have been given with your reinforcement tape. In fact, you are encouraged to do so—not only to look at different aspects of quitting, but also to prevent boredom.

Altering the reinforcement tape is simple. First, tailor the suggestions to your own needs, and write them down in script form. Be sure to make them simple, concise, and direct—that's how you'll achieve the best effects. Adapt your suggestions to help you meet particular problems and any foreseeable challenges to your quitting: "When I see my friend on Tuesday, I'm not going to have any problem in wanting a cigarette. I will feel relaxed, calm, and confident." That's the approach to take. Once you've got your suggestions in the form you want, make a new recording of the original script, just as you did before, but this time, substitute your own suggestions for those originally provided.

Reconsider the Benefits of Not Smoking— And Put Them To Good Use

It helps to reconsider the reasons you have become a nonsmoker, especially in the days immediately after participating in this three-hour program. *Really think* about each one of these important benefits; keep them perking in the forefront of your conscious thought. Use them as posthypnotic suggestions on your reinforcement tape when you are ready to alter the tape, or add them to the existing suggestions. What could be better motivation to stick to your commitment than all the good things you have bestowed on yourself?

To review, here are some of the obvious benefits you are now reaping as a nonsmoker:

The Benefits of Not Smoking

- Freedom from the nagging worry of the serious known health consequences of smoking: Cancer. Emphysema. Stroke. Heart attack.
- Clean, clear lungs, contributing to easier breathing, greater physical endurance, and stronger resistance to coughs, colds, and other respiratory ailments.
- Better blood circulation, encouraging a better, glowing complexion. More energy. More brain power and concentration.
- Cleaner, whiter teeth.
- Cleaner breath.

- Deeper, more restful sleep.
- A better response to sex.
- A new social image: A victorious example for family members, friends, children.
- A new social acceptance: Freedom of activity and ability to go anywhere, anytime. No more looks of disgust and irritation from others who do not smoke.
- A new feeling of personal pride, self-worth, and independence.
- A new sense of peace and liberation from a disabling habit.
- The power to do away with the inconvenience of it.
- Freedom from the expense. Just calculate what you save over the course of a year.
- More time to use your hands to help you relax. In the ten minutes it took to smoke a cigarette, you can now repot a plant, create a few rows of needlework, do woodcarving or beadwork. Or simply fold your hands, take a few deep breaths, and meditate. Pray. Relax.

The Reassuring Symptoms of Getting Well

About 70 percent of those people who stop smoking have few or no withdrawal symptoms; they manage very well, physically and mentally, in the days and weeks after they quit. We don't know exactly why others experience certain aftereffects—perhaps it has to do with the number of cigarettes they smoked, the degree to which they inhaled those cigarettes, or the pattern in which they smoked them. Whatever the causes, the physical symptoms of quitting (should they occur) are healthy, tangible signs that the body is recovering. In due course, these signs will disappear.

At first, some people cough up a little more mucus after quitting than they did when they smoked. Some people who rarely coughed when they smoked find they cough more once they have stopped smoking. This may seem alarming, but it is part of the cleanup and repair process underway in the respiratory system. The cough only occurs for a short time, until the mucus is gone.

Some people develop a slight sore throat for a few days, or develop a dry throat. It's all temporary and, again, part of the repair process; drinking liquids will help.

Some people become a bit light-headed in the days after they quit smoking. This is due to an increase in oxygen to the body—the *normal* amount of oxygen it needs.

Some people complain of lethargy, due to their pulse rate and blood pressure coming down—returning, again, to *normal* levels.

With a bad cold, you probably would feel a lot worse physically than you would ever feel withdrawing from cigarettes. The difference is that with a cold, you cannot escape the misery. You accept it because you have no choice. However, if you *do* experience any signs of withdrawal, you may find yourself thinking, *If I hadn't stopped smoking, none of these symptoms would be happening.* The reality is that if you hadn't *started* smoking, none (if any) of what is occurring now would have ever happened in the first place. Remember: You are not withdrawing from stopping smoking. You are withdrawing from *having smoked*.

Avoiding weight gain. The prospect of gaining large amounts of weight creates such anxiety among people who stop smoking that the facts covered in chapter 5 need to be emphasized once again: *With this program, you avoid significant weight gain*. We know our weight control guidelines really work because about 75 percent of those who participate in our group and private sessions do not put on any more than two or three pounds—almost no increase at all—and they readjust beautifully to the changes in their metabolism. To review, follow these simple guidelines:

First, understand that the metabolic rate slows down *to normal* after you quit, burning fewer calories than it did before, when smoking made it irregular. The adjustment here is simple—reduce the amount of any food you eat that contains flour or sugar and you will effectively and successfully keep your weight under control.

Second, understand that you are dealing with the sudden absence of a long-conditioned, automatic habit. As explained in chapter 5, if you smoked about twenty-five cigarettes a day, which is the usual amount for average smokers, you puffed on your cigarettes about two hundred fifty times a day. Without really thinking about it, you put something into your mouth about two hundred fifty times a day. In your mouth—*not* in your stomach. If you ate as much food as you smoked cigarettes, your weight gain would go off the charts! But remember: you don't have to let that habit of automatically putting a cigarette up to your mouth translate itself into putting food into your stomach. Or rationalize that you will reward yourself with food this week, and next week start to watch your weight. Instead, follow the suggestion given in chapter 5; drink lots of water; chew on a swizzle stick or coffee stirrer; eat a carrot stick or "free food" (see p. 60)—anything but candy, cake, cookies, or pizza. These temporary replacements will help you get used to the absence of all those cigarettes you put up to your mouth.

Third, and this relates back to your slowed metabolism in the days after you stop smoking: *By increasing your current level of physical activity, you can avoid gaining even one ounce.* Go beyond what you are used to doing. For example, if you never take walks, either for errands or enjoyment, then a brisk walk for ten or fifteen minutes a day is all it will take. Increase the time you swim or play tennis, if that's part of your routine. As a nonsmoker, you will naturally feel better increasing any physical activity you enjoy.

Last, and most important of all, use your new skill of self-hypnosis. Depend on it. Hypnosis has helped just as many people with controlling their weight as it has with quitting smoking. Now you have the means to exploit this powerful new force in your life by tailoring the suggestions on your reinforcement tape to your specific concerns. If gaining weight is one of them, your appetite will diminish rather than increase with hypnosis. You will have no food cravings; you will simply let them pass. Try it. Simple, clear hypnotic suggestions will work wonders for you in eliminating weight gain as a potential problem related to smoking.

There are other typical, minor changes you may experience.

Some new nonsmokers describe a certain awkwardness about what to do with their hands. They play imaginary drums, fold up paper, doodle with pens—all of that is perfectly fine. Have you ever changed over from driving a car with a stick shift to driving one with an automatic transmission? You are able to handle it, of course, but in the first few days after making the change, chances are you would find your left food going for the clutch every time you came to a light, and your right hand looking for the gear shift. That's a normal, temporary, automatic response.

From time to time, you may reach into your pocket or pocketbook, only to realize that you no longer smoke. Again, it's an automatic, harmless response, but one which underscores why you should never carry cigarettes around with you, even if it's just "so you have them." That's courting failure. There are so many times during the day that you could reach for one and smoke it without thinking, when that's so easy to avoid.

You may notice you sit differently, hold your hands

differently, even breathe differently. All are minor changes; it would be unusual if you didn't feel a bit out of synch in these first few days after giving up smoking. With the nonsmoking hypnotic suggestions on your reinforcement tape, you will have a great sense of control—the true, confident feeling of comfort and security that you can get through it without smoking. And thankfully, because of the hypnosis, it is not going to be that difficult to adjust to being a nonsmoker, and remaining one.

Psychological Withdrawal and How to Deal with It

Every individual who reads this book and participates in this program will have a different response. Some people will never want another cigarette again. They won't even think about it or have any problem whatsoever with the idea of never smoking. But don't be surprised if you find you think occasionally of a cigarette. Expect these thoughts. They are normal.

You would not be human if you never missed cigarettes after you quit. This is also perfectly normal, just as it is perfectly normal to feel somewhat depressed, nervous, or even just plain angry about it. All of these are natural coping tactics in dealing with a certain sense of loss.

You have time on your side—an important factor, which will be covered in more detail in chapter 10—but you also have hypnosis on your side. Hypnosis can help minimize or diminish your sense of loss by providing replacements—a sense of relaxed calm; a picture in focus of your own healthy body and the new life and energy that is coursing through it.

Don't be surprised if you still have thoughts about smoking twenty years after you've quit. Don't be scared if sometimes, you find yourself thinking, *Boy, would I love a cigarette*. As long as you can say to yourself, *But so what if I don't?* and go on with whatever you are doing, then you will be just fine.

Don't let the sudden thought of a cigarette *ever* surprise you, or make you anxious that you are weakening. If this initial stage of quitting passes without your ever once having a thought about smoking, and then suddenly, out of nowhere, you wake up one morning months from now and the first thing on your mind is a cigarette, you might think to yourself, *Uh-oh. Now it's wearing off; something's wrong*. But *nothing* is wrong. The thought of a cigarette might be there, initially, but your response has changed. *You are no longer a smoker.* That's what's important.

Regardless of how major or minor a role it played, *smoking was not something that in any way was positive in your life.* So while there is the thought of missing a cigarette, hypnosis now gives you the power to eliminate the craving for it. The fact that a thought occurs to you simply means you are in a situation in which you used to smoke. And if you go right on with what you are doing and take a long, slow, relaxing breath, that thought will effortlessly pass by.

Keep your goal of being a nonsmoker in focus as you move on to chapter 10 and conclude your reading. Remind yourself that many thousands of people with the same degree of motivation, will power, and good intentions as you have brought with you here today have surmounted temptations, emotions, and time—and have stopped smoking *forever*, using the program in this book.

10

Ensuring Your Long-Term Success as an Ex-Smoker

Mark Twain once said, "I don't see why people make such a fuss over quitting; I've done it thousands of times."

Well, you are going to prove Mr. Twain wrong. You will neither make *any* fuss—nor will you quit thousands of times! You have already done it. Once and for all, with no pain, anxiety, problems, or complications in your life.

If you go right on with what you are doing and take a long, slow, relaxed breath, the thought of a cigarette will effortlessly pass by. That last sentence of chapter 9 is probably one of the most important sentences in the book. It launches a powerful strategy you can depend on for achieving long-term success as an ex-smoker.

When you quit smoking on a moment-by-moment basis, going on with what you are doing and letting the thought of a cigarette pass, you are actually creating a new "passed" experience based exclusively on success. You are putting time on your side.

There is a very important reason to do this. Just as a reformed alcoholic recognizes there is no such thing as taking one drink—that one drink always leads to another, and eventually to getting drunk—so the successful ex-smoker realizes that there is no such thing as one cigarette. A few puffs and the nicotine is back into the system, along with the almost positive guarantee of going right back to the habit of smoking. Even without that craving, those who play the dangerous game of tempting fate with *What's the big deal? I'll just have one,* inevitably find themselves hooked once again, even though they may have quit for a long period of time.

So from this point forward—for the rest of your life, and in every circumstance that presents itself—you are going to use the moment, go right on with what you are doing, and let the thought of a cigarette pass. In other words, you will *always be in the present.*

Alcoholics Anonymous promotes a "one day at a time" philosophy—a proven means to build up confidence. As an ex-smoker, you can make the time frame even narrower than that. Thinking of forever—much less next week—is another dangerous game with quitting. Can you get through an hour without a cigarette? Of course you can. You've done it many times—in a meeting, in a movie, on the commuter train, and in a plane. It is not such a tremendous ordeal. *Forever* is an ordeal. So from now on, you are going to say to yourself, "I haven't smoked in a few hours; let's see how I can do for another hour without a cigarette." You will get through the hour, and therefore you will have won because *you have done what you said you would do.*

You will win, because you are free from worrying about problems that don't yet exist.

You don't anticipate them. The experts at failure tell themselves, "I *know* I can go all day without a cigarette, but after dinner, when I am having a cup of coffee, I *know* I'm going to need a cigarette. I *know* that I can't even get going when I first get up in the morning unless I have a cigarette." But you *don't know* it. All you know is that you can get through *right now.* What happens later today, or next week, or next month doesn't concern you because you live only in the present, telling yourself that regardless of what happens, you are not taking a cigarette. You are absolutely determined and committed to succeeding.

You will win, because you are free of the need to hope you will succeed.

As described earlier, some people go to sleep at night and say, "I am so tired; I couldn't sleep at all last night. But tonight I am going to sleep like a log." Other people say, "I am so tired; I couldn't sleep last night. I *hope* I can fall asleep tonight." And when they say the word "hope," it is not success they are implying; it is failure. Forget about hope. You will conquer smoking because you are absolutely committed to success.

You will win because you are stopping smoking for no one else but yourself.

Using someone else to give you motivation leads to playing games. You have an argument with them and then, "out of spite," you take a cigarette. Not only that, but you look at them and say, "Look what you made me do." Blaming another person for your going back to smoking is as silly as promising someone else you will quit, and then making his life miserable in hopes he'll relent and "give you permission" to smoke again. With these childish tactics, everyone loses. But you are not going to lose. You have accepted the responsibility for your decision to stop smoking, and you are not going to make yourself, or anyone else around you, miserable.

You will win because you have hypnosis working for you, freeing you from cravings and anxiety.

The success story is the person who crumples up his pack of cigarettes and throws it away, saying, "I don't care what happens; I am never taking another cigarette again." The failure story is the person who throws away the pack of cigarettes and says, "I hope this works," or "I'm going to try to stop smoking." You are not *trying* to quit. With hypnosis, you are doing it.

In five years, your body will fully recover and it will be as if you *never smoked* at all. You have given yourself this chance. When you close this book, determined and committed to succeed, you will be giving yourself the chance to stop smoking before you cause any permanent damage.

It does not make a bit of difference if you have tried to quit smoking before. With this book, you are giving yourself a better coaching job at long-term success than anything you have been doing. You have a new strategy. Not: I hope this works—let's see what happens. That's a terrible coaching job.

Instead, you are committed to making this program work—to giving it your all-out, full-blown commitment. And if you put in everything you've got, you will find that the hypnosis makes it easy. *Easy.* It gives you every ounce of control you need.

You made the commitment at the beginning of the book; now keep it alive in all the days to come. Use your hypnosis. You'll feel terrific as an ex-smoker.

Good Health and Good Luck!

About the Petrie Method

For over twenty-five years, the Petrie Method has been used to help hundreds of thousands of people take charge of their lives—offering programs for smoking cessation, weight control, stress management, fears and phobias, and other behavioral problems.

Seminars are offered at either the Institute for Hypnotherapy, with locations primarily in New York, New Jersey, and Connecticut, or through corporate programs given across the country.

The Petrie Metod has been featured on TV, in magazines, and in health journals.